GAY WARRIOR

D1500653

GAY WARRIOR

TRANSFORMING BETRAYAL INTO WISDOM

F. JIM FICKEY PhD
GARY S. GRIMM MA

A Guidebook for Gay Men of All Ages
Teaching the Principles of Initiation

GLB PUBLISHERS ®   San Francisco

Published in the United States by
GLB Publishers
P.O. Box 78212, San Francisco, CA 94107
www.GLBpubs.com

Cover Design by
GLB Publishers and the Authors

Library of Congress Cataloguing in Publication Data

Fickey, F. Jim, 1945-
  Gay warrior : transforming betrayal into wisdom / F. Jim Fickey, Gary S. Grimm.-- 1st ed.
      p. cm.
Includes bibliographical references and index.
  ISBN 1-879194-36-8 (alk. paper) -- ISBN 1-879194-37-6 (pbk. : alk. paper)
  1. Gay men--Psychology. 2. Gay men--Family relationships. 3. Gay men--Religious life. 4. Coming out (Sexual orientation) 5. Personality development. 6. Emotional maturity. 7. Interpersonal relations. I. Grimm, Gary S., 1957- II. Title.
HQ76 .F52 2002
305.38'9664--dc21
                    2002006577

1-879194-36-8 (Hardcover)
1-879194-37-6 (Paperback)
1-879194-38-4 (e-Book)

First printing   Sept., 2002
10 9 8 7 6 5 4 3 2 1

ACKNOWLEDGMENTS

We'd like to acknowledge the many gay men we've worked with throughout the years, and in particular, our group members, present and past, for returning each week to do the most difficult life work of all—committing to authenticity and awakening the Warrior.

We'd like to thank John Lee for his encouragement and belief in the project and valuable insight into how one gets a book published these days. Appreciation to Dan Jones for continuing to ask about the progress we were making. And to both, for their courage as straight men and comfort with their own sexuality, in honoring the Warrior in us.

Thanks to Bill Warner, our publisher, for saying yes.

And to all the people who have betrayed us. Even if we didn't know it at the time, you've been some of our greatest teachers.

For Randy —

    friend, colleague, fellow warrior

FOREWARD TO
GAY WARRIOR

I have been asked the same question on more than a few occasions, "Where do 'gay men' fit in this men's movement?" My answer is always the same, "Right beside Robert Bly, Sam Keen, Michael Meade and hundreds of other men who are participating in the men's movement's 'on the job training.'"

The next question one might ask, "When will it be SAFE enough?" My answer—"There is safety in numbers." *Gay Warrior* will hopefully find its way into a 'number' of hands that will reach out to each other, take them and together with their straight counterparts increase their pace and walk or even run quickly into the world of the "Deep Masculine."

I've been honored to work with men— "straight" and "gay" —for nearly twenty years. I know there are differences in our experiences, our strengths and our hopes. I've tried to honor those differences in the men's workshops, conferences and retreats that I've led or co-led. However, try as I might, the language, images, metaphors and examples were predominantly "heterosexual."

What Gary and Jim have done is speak to the gay man in a language that will feel true because they not only speak from experience and intellect but from the heart as well. While much of any man's journey into "true masculinity" is similar, the gay man's journey is fraught with obstacles, obnoxiousness, and pain the straight man can't even imagine, much less identify with. However, the gay man must make this often-perilous trek into the valleys and scale the mountains of manhood, but he does not have to do so alone and without company. This book makes a great companion on the journey.

Now gay men finally have a roadmap that has not existed before my friends wrote this book. I've worked with enough gay men to know that many need to wrestle away from the clutches of their mothers' arms, come to terms with the "absent father," and treat the "father-wound", deal with their addictions to substances, processes and perfectionism, move out of passivity and access their "warrior," all the while discovering their place and playing their unique role in the world of men, women and children.

The authors blend metaphors that have been keys to understanding and embracing the masculinity like "Iron John", "Puer" and others with the best work in the addictions field, along with material from great personal growth authors and renowned psychologists, stirring in plenty of case histories and personal experiences to produce a cornucopia that gay men can come to again and again to feed from and be nourished by during their journey.

I know Jim and Gary and have worked with them and visited with them over the years. They are great examples of men who want to heal their wounds and claim their rightful place by those many men who are trying to make it a safer world for all men, women and children to live in, and most importantly they are "walking their talk", falling down like the rest of us on occasion, brushing themselves off and taking another step into their own masculinity. Therefore it is a great privilege and honor to write this brief foreward for them, with hope that gay men will turn the pages of this wonderful book, and if not see themselves on every page, then at least see men they have loved or are yet to love.

I wrote a book a long time ago called *The Flying Boy: Healing the Wounded Man* (Health Communications Inc. 1987) and one of the best compliments I ever received came from a gay man. He sat down on a pillow in my office and I pulled up another and sat beside him. He looked me in the eyes and said, "I read your book and I felt that I could tell you the truth because you were so honest and truthful. You told me about your pain and how you have tried to heal your woundedness around being a male and coming to terms with your father, your relationships and your life. I know you are a heterosexual and where you said 'she' I put 'he' and the book worked just fine for me." If I didn't admit that I didn't say many times, "Wow, I can relate to this and that and say a number of times 'me too'" while reading *Gay Warrior,* I'd be less than honest and truthful. This is an honest book, written for gay men by gay men, but it spoke to me and I learned from it—about myself and about gay men. With this said, I hope this wonderful book finds its way into as many men's hands as possible—straight or gay. We all need to know each other and ourselves as best we can. This book and the authors help us do just that. My prayer and hope is that some day men will say things like, "Oh, I have these friends—Gary and Jim…" or "I have this friend, John," and forget to say these "gay friends" or "straight friend" and we will be friends, brothers, colleagues and companions on the road to health, wholeness, and continue to deepen our ability to love each other.

—John Lee, author of the best-selling *The Flying Boy: Healing the Wounded Man, Facing The Fire: Experiencing and Expressing Anger Appropriately* and his most recent book, *Growing Yourself Back Up: Understanding Emotional Regression.* John is the Founder and Former Director of The Austin Men's Center.

CONTENTS

PART I

INTRODUCTION

Who are we as 21st-century gay men, and what is our purpose at this time on the planet? Although there is no simple answer to these questions, three things appear to be certain:

One: Gay men have a deep soul-longing to live as powerful adults, to share their creativity with their world and to make meaningful connections.
Two: Most gay men have suffered an inordinate amount of betrayal that has left them deeply wounded.
Three: If their wounds remain unhealed, gay men will be unable to reach their full potential as strong adults.

In working with hundreds of gay men over many years, we have identified certain types of betrayals specific to the gay experience—from society, our families, and then, ultimately, self-betrayal. The purpose of this book is to help gay men understand how their betrayals influence their behavior, their relationships, the decisions they make and the perceptions they hold. Once learned, they can begin to transform their betrayals into a source of wisdom.

As well, *Gay Warrior* is designed to teach the principles of Initiation, an ancient practice that helps people move from a place of adolescence into adulthood and to live as more powerful adults— whom we call *Warriors*. Once gay men understand how certain patterns of behavior and perceptions actually prevent them from living as *Warriors*, they will have a much better chance at developing new, healthier ways of expressing their true spiritual nature.

As a cautionary note, this book may, at times, be difficult for some men to read. Although we hope that *Gay Warrior* will help our readers to ultimately feel better about themselves, this is not a "feel good" book. Our challenge, as writers, has been to let *our* Warriors speak. We have attempted to tell the truth as we see it. Sometimes our truth may be hard to hear, but if it resonates, try it. It may not be everyone's truth. That's okay. Our intention is to help gay men find their own truth, whether it coincides with ours or not. What we hope is that the reader will keep an open mind to the ideas presented here as possibilities for growth and expanded consciousness. *Gay Warrior* is intended to help men identify what is not working in their lives and to learn how to change patterns that keep them stuck. Confronting core issues can be painful; it can also be one of the most direct paths to transformation. In Scott Peck's *The Road Less Traveled*, his very first sentence is, "Life is difficult" (p. 15). In keeping with that spirit, *this book is difficult.*

This book is written to help gay men become free—psychologically, spiritually, and politically. Finding the *Warrior* is the only way we know to attain such freedom. In order to accomplish such a task, gay men must be willing to relinquish certain beliefs and behaviors that may be familiar, and thus comfortable, to them.

Gay Warrior is a compilation of our years of work with an enormous variety of gay men—many of them courageous *Warriors* in their own right. We have been fortunate to witness the Initiation work of many of these men who have been, and continue to be, willing to transform their betrayals into wisdom through a deep process work that ultimately leads to the emergence of their *Warrior*.

As psychotherapists, we see gay men becoming increasingly more dissatisfied with the stereotypes placed on them—*from within and outside* their community—and society's attempt to keep them boy-like. They are men who desire to live more consciously and are questioning the value of our youth-driven culture. Many are yearning to find more emotional and spiritual depth in their lives. They want to be powerful men, but don't necessarily know how to become so. We believe gay men long for Initiation.

Even if they're not familiar with the terminology, the desire to grow up, to be taken seriously, and to be treated with equality and respect, runs deep within them.

The greatest challenge for a gay man in finding his *Warrior* is in learning how he reacts from his unhealed betrayals, and how he remains unconsciously committed to not growing up. The book is a guide to help gay men of all ages and backgrounds better understand what it means to be gay and powerful, and what we can accomplish once we embrace our power. The future health and well being of the gay community and of the planet depends on our ability to become strong and powerful *Warriors*.

There is a still, small voice deep within the collective unconscious of gay men beginning to emerge. Twenty years ago this voice was a mere whisper. Today, many gay men seem to be aware of its presence and are consciously working to decipher its message. For those who are listening, this voice is a reminder of a greater potentiality in each of us. It tells us that our gayness is not some cosmic accident or genetic mutation, but rather a spiritual gift that we can either choose to develop or squander.

In short, we gay men are here for a specific reason. We are here to help heal this planet, but in order to do so we must first heal ourselves. This book is an offering to gay men everywhere who are in search of such healing.

Jim Fickey

http://www.gaywarrior.com   Gary Grimm

June, 2002

A bit of advice
Given to a young Native American
At the time of his initiation:

"As you go the way of life,
you will see a great chasm.
Jump.
It is not as wide as you think."
(from *A Joseph Campbell Companion,* p. 26)

THE WARRIOR

Since we cannot go back to the womb or infancy, we must grow up.
We can only go forward through the desert of life,
making our way painfully over parched and barren ground
into increasingly deeper levels of consciousness.
—from *Further Along the Road Less Traveled,* M. Scott Peck, p. 19.

The Warrior is an archetype within the unconscious of all men that contains his truth, fierceness and wisdom. All gay men have a Warrior, though for most he remains in an embryonic stage. For very specific reasons that we will discuss shortly, many gay men have never found their Warrior. For them, this power source exists out of their reach, relegated to some distant realm, a vague notion of masculinity, an undefined whisper of thought just beyond conscious awareness. Even if a gay man has only a limited understanding of the concept, he may have felt at some point in his life a nagging sense of something missing in his masculinity, some piece of his manhood not yet discovered. We believe this missing piece to be the Warrior, and when the gay man finds him, he is able to live with more integrity and discernment. He is able to take healthier risks and to welcome challenges, knowing this is how to live as a powerful adult. He is able to stand firm in his truth and share with his world the wisdom he has acquired from having traveled an arduous path. Most importantly, when a gay man finds his Warrior he is able to transform his betrayals into wisdom.

Until gay men find their Warrior, on a personal level as well as a collective one, we will continue to be viewed by much of society as second-class citizens, a group that does not have to be taken seriously. We will continue to be denied equal rights protection, denied tax and insurance benefits afforded straight people, prevented from marrying, adopting children, and discriminated against in the work place. We will even be fired from our jobs on the basis of our sexual orientation without recourse. One of the main reasons we have not yet attained these equal rights may be that most gay men have not yet found their Warrior. If more had, we would have said a long time ago, "We will not tolerate such injustice any longer."

This voice of righteous indignation, another aspect of the Warrior, is beginning to be expressed, but our journey to freedom has just begun.

Iron John, written by Robert Bly, an American poet, philosopher and visionary, is one of the most important works thus far written regarding the Warrior. In this groundbreaking book, Bly describes the Warrior as, "a large man covered with hair from head to foot" (p. 5). Indeed, the Warrior is a wild beast—extremely powerful. He can even be fierce if necessary, a destroyer.

We want to take a moment here to say a few words about our choice of the term Warrior. Although some people have asked us along the way why we deliberately chose a word that *can* connote aggression and war, we decided a long time ago in writing this book that Warrior was the very term that best applied to the principles of Initiation that we want gay men to learn about. When we use the term, we are not advocating aggression or violence; rather we are inviting gay men to reconnect with a power source deep within them that can be fierce and vital to their very survival.

As well, we believe it necessary to differentiate between two different kinds of Warrior: the "positive" Warrior and the "shadow" Warrior. The shadow Warrior is an out-of-control energy within some men that is responsible for the extreme violence happening in our society today—the World Trade Center, Columbine High School, the Matthew Shephard murder, road rage, domestic violence and the senseless brutality we are reminded of everyday on the evening news. At no time in this book are we condoning such negative Warrior behavior. We are not encouraging gay men to become Rambos; rather we are encouraging them to find their positive mature masculine. Bly explains this well:

> We have to accept the possibility that the true radiant energy in the male does not hide in, reside in, or wait for us in the feminine realm, nor in the macho/John Wayne realm, but in the magnetic field of the deep masculine…the kind of wildness, or un-niceness, implied by the Wild Man image [or archetype] is not the same as macho energy [but rather] leads to forceful action undertaken, not with cruelty, but with resolve. (p. 8)

The positive Warrior's purpose, on the other hand, is to think for himself, to question. He knows how to fight; and he fights *for* his most cherished beliefs, *against* whatever may stand in the way of his truth. Furthermore, the positive Warrior is not the same as a soldier (more often associated with the shadow Warrior). The soldier's purpose is to obey orders; he is discouraged from thinking for himself.

Herein lies the main difference between the positive Warrior and the shadow Warrior.

> The Warrior is often a destroyer. But the positive Warrior energy destroys only what needs to be destroyed in order for something new and fresh, more alive and virtuous, to appear. Many things in our world need destroying—corruption, tyranny, oppression, injustice, obsolete and despotic systems of government.... And in the very act of destroying, often the Warrior energy is building new civilizations, new artistic and spiritual ventures for humankind, new relationships. (*King, Warrior, Magician, Lover,* p.86).

When a gay man comes out, for example, he is acting as a destroyer. He is destroying the fantasy that he and others have previously lived with—the fantasy of his being someone other than who he really is. Such destruction is vital to the well-being of this man, and is a function of the positive Warrior.

Within Jungian psychology, the Warrior is one of the four major archetypes comprising the mature masculine—the psychological state within every man representing complete adulthood. An archetype is an energy force found within the unconscious. It is a universal symbol that appears in all cultures throughout history.

In their book *King, Warrior, Magician, Lover: Rediscovering the Archetypes of the Mature Masculine,* Robert Moore and Douglas Gillette skillfully define each of the facets of the mature masculine, or what they call "Man Psychology."

The King Archetype represents the wisdom of a man. "[This] archetype in its fullness possesses the qualities of order, or reasonable and rational patterning, of integration and integrity in the masculine psyche," (p. 61). The King has the power of inner authority, and is that part of a man that provides ordering and blessing. As well, the King is generative. For straight men, this generativity may manifest through offspring. For gay men, generativity more often occurs through our work and our contributions to our communities.

The Magician..."is the archetype of thoughtfulness and reflection," (p. 108). If men are not in contact with their Magician energy, they will often be passive-aggressive and lack a sense of inner security. The realm of the

Magician includes careers that take special training where one must study diligently to become a master of his profession. The shamans of indigenous cultures had Magician energy. Interestingly, these shamans were often gay men, as evidenced by the *berdache* of the Native American communities.

The Lover archetype "...is the primal energy pattern of...vividness, aliveness and passion," (p. 120). The Lover is able to empathize with his world, and thus is in touch with the pain of the world. "Painters, musicians, poets, sculptors, and writers are often 'mainlining' the Lover. The artist is well known to be sensuous and sensual," (p.129). Important to note that, of all the archetypes, most gay men seem to be most connected to their Lover archetype. (More is said about this in PART V: The Warrior Relationship.)

Of all four archetypes of the mature masculine, it is our belief that most gay men are least in touch with their Warrior. It is for this reason that we focus our attention on the characteristics of the Warrior (as well as the characteristics of what we deem to be the antithesis of the Warrior—the *Puer*) in order to help gay men more fully develop their mature masculine.

Later in the book, we will look at specific Warrior behaviors and attitudes that will help gay men to incorporate this archetypal energy force into their everyday lives. For now, it is important to define a few more concepts: *Puer* and Initiation.

THE *PUER*

"It was because I heard father and mother," he explained in a low voice, "talking about what I was to be when I became a man." He was extraordinarily agitated now. "I don't want ever to be a man," he said with passion. "I want always to be a little boy and to have fun. So I ran away to Kensington Gardens and lived a long long time with the fairies," (*Peter Pan*, p. 29).

The *Puer* is the opposite of the Warrior; it is the archetype within every man that represents his eternal youth. The *Puer* (pronounced *poo-air*) is the psychological component of a gay man that still behaves, thinks and reacts to his world like a child, and it is the same part that most often keeps him from being able to fully embrace his manhood. As with Peter Pan, a familiar character for many of us from childhood, the *Puer* expresses the same longing—to never grow up. When a gay man has not healed his betrayals, he remains a *Puer*. Clearly, there are many gay men out there who are definite *Puers*.

Understanding the role of the *Puer*, and its myriad liabilities, is one of the most important challenges that any gay man will face before he is able to become a truly empowered adult. This archetypal force can hinder his ability to sustain intimate relationships and prevent him from succeeding in work. It can adversely affect his self-esteem and encourage others not to take him seriously. It can lead to disempowerment and disconnection from his world, and even motivate him to engage in life-threatening behaviors jeopardizing his physical, emotional and spiritual well being.

While some gay men have been able to grow up successfully and let go of their *Puer*, moving into a place of genuine adulthood, most gay men are caught in the throes of this powerful energy force. Sadly, many are motivated by their *Puer* on an unconscious level, never knowing how this archetype influences their social, personal, and professional interactions. To better understand the *Puer*, let us explain where the term comes from, what its psychological implications are, and how it affects gay men on a day-to-day basis.

Carl Jung first introduced the term *Puer* into modern-day psychology, taking it from Greek mythology where *Puer Aeternus* was the child god, the eternal youth who never grew up. From a Jungian perspective, the *Puer* is an archetypal force within every man that wants to remain a child (for women, this archetype is known as the *Puella*). Other psychologists since Jung, like Marie Louise von Franz and Heinz Kohut have expanded the concept of the *Puer*. As von Franz states, "...the man who is identified with the archetype of the *puer aeternus* remains too long in adolescent psychology; that is, all those characteristics that are normal in a youth of seventeen and eighteen are continued into later life." (von Franz, p. 1).

Most people function out of a variety of ego states, depending on the situation and their degree of Initiation, that is, their level of adulthood. (We will discuss the concept of Initiation in more depth in the following chapter.) Eric Berne, *Transactional Analysis in Psychotherapy*, identified three main ego states that he labeled the Parent, the Adult, and the Child. The parent ego state is similar to Freud's Superego and while an important concept, we will limit our discussion to the differences between the Adult and the Child. For purposes of clarification, we include in the Child category the adolescent stage of development, since this is specifically what the *Puer* represents. Therefore, in keeping with the historic definition of the *Puer* as both the child god and the divine youth, we will use the term *Puer* to represent both the Inner Child and the Inner Adolescent.

Robert Moore and Douglas Gillette use a little different terminology. What we will call *Puer* psychology, they call boy psychology. Men, who are fixated at an immature level of development, are merely grown boys. Examples of such men are:

> The drug dealer, the ducking and diving political leader, the wife beater, the chronically "crabby" boss, the "hot shot" junior executive, the unfaithful husband, the company "yes man," the indifferent graduate school adviser, the "holier than thou" minister, the gang member, the father who can never find the time to attend his daughter's school programs, the coach who ridicules his star athletes, the therapist who unconsciously attacks his clients' "shining" and seeks a kind of gray normalcy for them, the yuppie—all these men have something in common. They are all boys pretending to be men (p. 13).

The more initiated a person is, the more often he will function out of his Adult and/or (nurturing) Parent ego state. The less initiated he is, the more he will function out of his Child/Adolescent ego state. Psychologists and psychotherapists have begun to understand the pervasive nature of *Puer* psychology within contemporary society. We are just beginning to recognize how the *Puer* inhibits a person's ability to become an adult—and more specifically, the gay man's.

We feel it is important to note here that the *Puer* also contains positive qualities. Such qualities include idealism, creativity, spontaneity, and a sense of adventure. The *Puer* helps us to fantasize, daydream, be goofy, act impulsively, and get "crazy". Examples of this could include enjoying sports, playing music, painting, sculpting, crafting, roller-blading, hang-gliding, sky diving—anything that would fall into the category of having fun.

Conversely, the negative qualities of the *Puer* include addiction, narcissism, disconnection, and irresponsibility. They include the aspects in each of us that are not interested in the daily and ordinary; the unsensational responsibilities of life, relationship and work.

The problem of the *Puer*, for the gay man, begins when he spends the majority of his time living as a child, allowing the *Puer* to be in the driver's seat of his psychological world. The *Puer* cannot successfully navigate through the adult world; he does not understand it, nor does he have much interest in learning about it. The idea of assuming the responsibilities of adulthood may strike him as being not only abhorrent, but unnecessary as well. When the gay man lives primarily in the *Puer* stage, we refer to such a condition as being "stuck" in one's *Puer*.

When a gay man gets stuck in his *Puer*, this archetypal force guides him through life, influencing the most important decisions he makes—whether they relate to work, relationships, money, sex, spirituality, or politics. Invariably, a man led by his *Puer* will live in a world of fantasy and illusion. Such a world, however seductive, provides a shaky foundation on which to accomplish the goals of adulthood. The gay man often has a strong and abiding, albeit unconscious, allegiance to his *Puer*.

On the surface, functioning out of the Inner Adolescent ego state can look like the ultimate freedom. The *Puer* has few responsibilities and is accountable to no one. He would rather pursue his false sense of specialness and importance than to live as a mere mortal.

The *Puer* prefers to play, avoiding monotonous and routine work whenever possible, and often engages in intense, yet short-lived, romantic involvement. Soon tiring of a sexual partner, he moves on to the next person. Underneath this seeming freedom, the consequences of remaining a *Puer* can include an inability to: connect to one's world, genuinely care for others, or truly commit to someone or something; and a difficulty in staying in one place long enough to find home.

In Part III: How We Betray Ourselves, we explore the various *Puer* patterns we have found to be the most common within the gay experience. This exploration is designed to help the gay man better understand how his particular *Puer* expresses itself. The *Puer* has many facets and so must be explored from a variety of angles. To paraphrase John Bradshaw, there are a lot of adolescents (i.e. *Puers*) out there running around in adult bodies. Within gay culture, there seems to be a preponderance of these *Puers*.

Note: Within both Jungian and psychoanalytic theory, the *Puer* is viewed as the same as the narcissist. Although this theory has merit, (we include in Part III information on the narcissist), we believe that much of the *Puer* behaviors and attitudes found within gay culture are the result of gay men's lack of Initiation rather than just unhealed narcissism. In keeping with this premise, we have found that when gay men are able to complete their adolescent stage of development and move successfully into adulthood, many of their *Puer* characteristics begin to diminish.

Let's now look at the concept of Initiation, the process by which any of us can let go of the *Puer*.

INITIATION

When we can no longer deny we are gay and can no longer stand silent about the lies we were told and had swallowed, we come out of the closet and enter the "Separating" stage. It is here that we assert ourselves as *gay gladiators* [italics ours] and do battle with the attitudes of family, the Church, lawmakers, the press and others who say bad things about being gay.
— Brian McNaught, *On Being Gay*, p. 34.

For the gay man to become a Warrior, a fully self-actualized adult, and to let go of his *Puer*, he must embark on the journey of Initiation. Initiation refers to the ritualized process that a person experiences which marks a definite ending to his boyhood and a clear beginning of his manhood. It is his rite of passage.

Essential to all Initiation is separating from one's family of origin, in particular, letting go of the fantasy bond with Mom and Dad. Initiation is about cutting the psychic umbilical cord that continues to connect the son to his parents. For many gay men, that cord sometimes stays firmly attached well into their 30's, 40's and beyond. Such a condition may have dire consequences, for they will never be able to fully mature and have a life of their own. The process of cutting that cord can be a painful one, but the rewards are great—including increased personal power and freedom.

Integral to a gay man's journey of Initiation is to learn how to transform betrayal into wisdom. In order to do so, he needs to be willing to acknowledge how and by whom he has been betrayed, and then to begin to feel whatever emotions might not have been worked through regarding those betrayals.

Indigenous cultures have understood the importance of Initiation and have practiced various forms of it for thousands of years. Whether we look to African or Australian tribes or to Native Americans, we can still find the practice of Initiation. It begins when the young boy, usually around the age of puberty, is taken from his family and placed in the care of the older men, the elders, to learn the ways of the tribe and to come to a greater understanding of himself as a man. During this time, he learns the stories and customs of his people: their songs, dances, rituals and mythology. He learns practical things—hunting, fishing, building—that will help him to survive and be a contributing member of his community.

Eventually, at the end of this training, he is sent out into the wilds on a "vision quest." As seen in the young aborigine of Papua New Guinea, he goes off into the jungle for many days alone, given no food to take on his journey. This journey might include the use of some hallucinogenic substance to offer him a more profound connection to the spirit world. Having nothing but himself to rely on, he learns that he can and must take care of himself.

This vision quest forces the boy to shed his old skin, the skin of youth, and thus helps him to learn what it means to be a man. When he is finished, he has developed a new perception of himself—a man with a place within his tribe. It is important to note that, basically, everyone survives the Initiation, even though the implication is that there is a potential for failure. But that failure, which increases the seriousness of the task, is more perceived than actual. Certainly the process is dangerous, but the purpose of Initiation is to ultimately strengthen the tribe, not destroy it.

When he finishes this journey, he is initiated. In other words, he has become a man. Afterward, he may return to his family, but he will be treated differently. His family will treat him with the respect due any other man of the tribe. He may wear different clothes, have been circumcised or tattooed, and/or have a new name—all symbols of his passage from boyhood into manhood.

Initiation rituals vary from one tribe to the next, but they occur, in some form, within most indigenous cultures. For instance, within the Native American tribes of the southwest, initiation rituals are still practiced today. Young boys are taken from their families and placed in the kiva, (a circular space underground, where all life originates), to learn how to become men.

Through anthropological research, we Westerners have learned the purpose and value of Initiation, and are now beginning to realize that the so-called "primitive" peoples of the world have much to teach us about becoming adults. As well, we are sensing the consequences for those of us living in a society that lacks formalized Initiation rituals.

■ ■ ■

In 1908, Arnold van Gennep wrote the book, *The Rites of Passage*. He explains male rites of passage as occurring in three phases: *separation, transition, and incorporation*. *Separation* is literal; the young boy is actually separated from his former life. He is taken from the security of his mother's and younger sibling's world and forced to join the unknown world of his father and uncles. The boy must sever his ties with the comfortable and familiar world of the feminine. *The boy must die for the man to be born.*

Transition is the second phase and it is more often a period of seclusion, hazing (a physical and/or mental ordeal), and deprivation. The boy must learn adult survival and the affirmation of manhood. Frequently, the boy's name is changed during this period to further assist in his evolving status. "The transition phase redefines the physical, social, and spiritual existence of its participants…the past is ritualistically laid to rest, for the insecurities of childhood must be banished forever" (Raphael, p.7).

The final phase is *incorporation*. The young man, no longer a boy, is finally accepted into the larger societal structure as an adult male. This is the cumulative effect of the initiative process, "the transformation from the weakness and vulnerability of childhood to the strength and self-confidence required of manhood" (p.12). This theme of death and rebirth, so fundamental for one to find manhood, is largely missing from our society.

Ray Raphael, in *The Men from the Boys*, explains that all the substitutes we have for male initiation in our culture lack at least one of these important phases. Many modern day replacements involve separation, such as: graduation from high school, first job, marriage and travel. Some may include transition: college, fraternity rituals, armed forces, combat or internships; but none of them contains all three phases of the initiation ritual which are necessary to accomplish the difficult task of turning boys into men. It is the final phase, incorporation, that is often missing from these examples.

There is a deep, primordial longing within all men to become initiated. Susan Faludi talks of the betrayal of the American man, and points time and again to the absence of Initiation for American men and their quest to find it. For example, the Promise Keepers Movement, which drew millions of members during the mid-90's, worked on the promise of providing Initiation to its members. Faludi cites Gordon Dalbey's book, *Fight Like a Man*, considered one of the bibles of the movement. Dalbey talks about the importance of Initiation by placing it within the context of religion and God the father. However much we disagree with this idea, he is appealing to one of man's deepest longings: to become strong.

Until we develop an understanding of the importance of Initiation, both on the personal and the collective level, we will continue to choose *uninitiated* men (and women) to lead us, we will tolerate their *Puer* behavior, which will in turn reinforce our own skewed sense of adulthood. As long as we remain uninitiated, we will have difficulty finding and sustaining adult relationships, and in particular, love relationships. Becoming initiated helps us to turn our sense of allegiance from our parents to our adult world. Until we break free from our allegiance to our parents, our partners won't stand a chance.

In our work with gay men, we've come to recognize some common themes regarding Initiation. These themes, or common threads, are woven into the fabric of each man's journey and are, in fact, challenges that gay men must face in order to become truly adult. Of these challenges, the most important is in learning how to heal the betrayals specific to the gay experience. In the next chapter, we will begin to examine those betrayals. Later we will discuss in more depth the major betrayals that gay men must confront in order to heal and become more fully adult.

PART II

BETRAYAL OF THE GAY MAN

Most gay men, no matter what their age or cultural background, have experienced an inordinate amount of betrayal starting at a very early age. Our parents were usually the first to betray us—not knowing how to effectively deal with our "differentness." Perhaps they even pretended that we weren't different from our siblings, even though everyone in our world, on some level, knew we were. It might have started when Dad, sensing there was something different about us, began to pull away, started to spend less time with us.

Betrayal continued once we started school. We may have begun to be singled out, taunted unmercifully, called names like sissy, homo, or queer; maybe we were the last to be picked for a team sport, told we threw like a girl, were the brunt of fag jokes or made fun of and humiliated by the other boys in the locker room.

It wasn't just our peers who betrayed us. There was also the occasional teacher doing a pretty thorough job. The one who shamed us in front of our classmates or who allowed our classmates to do so without intervening on our behalf. There might have also been the closeted teacher who inadvertently reinforced our sense of shame and confusion by remaining silent. If only they had had the courage to somehow take us aside and tell us that being gay was okay, what a profound difference they could have made in our lives. They would have provided a safe haven for us in what was often a hostile environment.

Further betrayal happened when, in high school, "heterosexual privilege" allowed our straight peers to experiment and learn about courtship rituals, while we were left merely to dream of what it might be like to experience physical and sexual intimacy.

We were betrayed in places of worship when we heard the minister or priest or rabbi condemning homosexuality, and understanding in some vague, and yet unarticulated way, that it was *us* he was referring to.

Betrayal continues into present time when we are the victims of a hate crime, or a rejecting homophobic family. We are betrayed by a society that continues to "infantilize" us—to keep us child-like and disempowered by refusing us equal rights protections, denying us the same tax breaks, insurance/inheritance benefits afforded straight couples, and invalidating our marriages. Clearly, as long as gay men (and women) remain second-class citizens, and are perceived as having less value, we will never be a threat to the existing social order. Mainstream America won't have to take us seriously or view us as a socio-political force to be reckoned with.

We are infantilized by gay culture as well. Daily, gay culture bombards us with messages that tell us: *Don't Grow Up!* Youth worship pervades gay magazines, art, literature, and can be experienced first hand at the gym, bars, beach, and is epitomized within the "circuit" culture.

Seldom are gay men of any age ever taught the importance of maturing—physically, psychologically, or spiritually. Without such instruction, we lack the guidance for knowing how to become powerful adults and visionary elders. So how do we gay men become more powerful, self-actualized adults, when both mainstream culture and our gay subculture encourage us at almost every turn, to remain boy-like?

Without guidance, we don't. We remain adolescents in adult bodies. One of the ultimate betrayals of all.

■   ■   ■

Sadly, many gay men have not done their work and eventually succumb to their betrayals. Over the course of a lifetime, they develop a certain edge or cynicism toward life and themselves that is more about a well-concealed victim than an empowered adult. An example of such an edge is the bitchy, campy humor that gay men are so famous for. It is a type of humor that is a passive aggressive expression of unowned and unacknowledged anger and sadness. Bitchiness is one of the defenses gay men use to deal with their betrayal when they haven't learned other, healthier options.

Given the amount and duration of betrayal that most gay men have suffered, we could, theoretically, become some of the strongest Warriors within our society. But *only* if we've done our work to heal the deep and traumatic wounding caused by our cumulative betrayals. If we don't heal our wounds, chances are we will move further into a victim place, where we withdraw from our world and become more afraid, angry, and mistrusting.

In the following pages, we examine how gay men can do the healing work necessary to become stronger, healthier adults. We explain how, through Initiation, a gay man can learn to turn his deepest emotional wounds into a source of great power and strength. In the next chapters, we discuss two of the potentially most profound betrayals of all—betrayal by Mother and Father. This investigation is not for the purpose of vilifying or blaming these people. Rather it is to help the gay man understand the specific ways that his parents might have impaired his ability to live as a fully empowered adult. As well, its purpose is to help him break the fantasy bond that may be keeping him a little boy.

SEBASTIAN AND VIOLET:
VIOLET AND SEBASTIAN

The Importance of Divorcing Our Mothers

I'm going up to see the captain now. Tell him to change our course for home. Oh, Sebastian. What a lovely summer it's been. Just the two of us. Sebastian and Violet. Violet and Sebastian. Just the way it's always going to be. Oh, we are lucky, my darling. To have one another, and need no one else—ever.
— *Suddenly Last Summer*, Tennessee Williams.

A mother betrays her gay son when she develops and maintains an unhealthy and inappropriately close emotional relationship with him, uses him as a surrogate husband and/or refuses to let him "divorce" her. As with Violet Venable, who maintains a kind of psychotic delusion of her son/lover, any mother who clings so tenaciously to her gay son for her emotional security can, in the end, destroy him.

For the gay man to become a Warrior, he must at some point in his life divorce his mother. This divorce is arguably the single, most difficult challenge he will face in becoming initiated. Not only may he be faced with his mother's unwillingness to let go of him, but also his *Puer* may make such a task all the more daunting. The *Puer's* survival is dependent on the maintenance of the fantasy bond with Mother. Such a fantasy provides him with the false comfort and illusion that he and his mother are bound together in some mystical and indescribable way that bares an uncanny resemblance to actual marriage. Such a marriage, if not consciously terminated will wreak havoc in a gay man's life, and prevent him from ever being able to claim his manhood.

According to Marie-Louise von Franz, for the *Puer* such a divorce would shatter his sense of specialness and false individuality that the fantasy bond encourages. The whole notion of divorcing mother threatens the *Puer's* existence. Divorcing the mother requires the adult to let go of the fantasy bond that the *Puer* clings to with tenacity; the mere mention of such an idea can throw him into a state of abject panic. Divorcing the mother is a multi-faceted process of individuation and usually begins with coming out to her, but it does not end there.

A man's relationship to his mother—no matter how close or distant—holds a place of special significance. For the gay man, his relationship to his mother may have an even greater and unparalleled significance. Because of its importance, it behooves the gay man to more fully understand and explore how this relationship has shaped who he is today and how it has aided or hindered him in his development. Equally important, he must come to see how it may be the thing keeping him stuck and unable to find his power, his manhood.

The difficulty in such an exploration, at least therapeutically, seems to result from the level of sacredness that many gay men attach to this relationship. So sacred, it can make such an exploration off-limits. In therapy it is often met with a high degree of resistance. This resistance is understandable since, for many gay sons, their mothers have been their salvation. Growing up, the gay son may have sought refuge in the company of his mother. She may have been his safe haven. And for this, rightfully so, he might feel a profound sense of gratitude. For many gay sons, their mothers were their main support.

Nevertheless, one of the greatest obstacles that all gay men must overcome in order to become a Warrior is to relinquish their allegiance to their mothers. In short, they must be willing to let go of the emotional and psychic attachment to them. The level of resistance to this concept that we've encountered in our work with gay men has warranted giving it a special name, "The Violet and Sebastian Syndrome."

This name, taken from Tennessee Williams' play *Suddenly Last Summer*, is one of the most poignant literary examples of what happens when a gay son is unable to divorce his mother. With a keen eye for revealing the inner workings of the human psyche, and in particular, the relationship between mothers and sons, Williams understood the potential for emotional incest between a mother and a gay son. More importantly, he understood the destructive nature of such a relationship when the gay son remains the mother's fantasy lover.

Williams describes the relationship between a domineering mother, Violet Venable, and her deceased, gay son, Sebastian. As the story unfolds, the relationship, as described through the very narcissistic lens of Violet, takes on almost unrivaled Oedipal proportions. She recounts to the young doctor, with unnerving fervor and pride:

My son, Sebastian, demanded! We were a famous couple. People didn't speak of Sebastian and his mother or Mrs. Venable and her son, they said "Sebastian and Violet, Violet and Sebastian are staying at the Lido, they're at the Ritz in Madrid. Sebastian and Violet, Violet and Sebastian have taken a house at Biarritz for the season," and every appearance, every time we appeared, attention was centered on *us!—everyone else eclipsed!* Vanity? Ohhhh, no, Doctor, you can't call it that (p.12).

The play gets more excruciatingly intense as the mother's pathology and distorted memories spill out revealing a level of dysfunction that can make even the most trained therapist quiver. It is a relationship of emotional incest, blurred boundaries, betrayal and eventual death. It is a character study, brilliantly constructed, that captures the poignancy and pathos of a mother/gay son dynamic—a dynamic that we, as therapists, encounter time after time. It is a dynamic that, for the gay son, if left unchecked, can lead to despair, loneliness, and ultimate death (if not literal, then certainly emotional and spiritual death).

Until a gay man divorces his mother, one or both can live in a fantasy that they have a certain type of lover relationship, not unlike the fantasy that Violet creates. Rollo May, in a conversation with Sam Keen, explains this situation in the following way, "The dilemma of the modern son is that he *wins* the Oedipal battle against the father and gets Mother. And then he doesn't know what to do with her because she overwhelms him" (Keen, p.20).

The fantasy lover relationship between a gay man and his mother rarely occurs on a conscious level; rather, it gets played out more often on a deep, unconscious level, where the dynamic can be so subtle, so insidious, it is hard to identify. Such a fantasy lover relationship exists in a variety of forms. Let's take a closer look at some of them.

First and foremost, a fantasy lover relationship (The Violet and Sebastian Syndrome) has the most chance of flourishing when a gay son has not yet come out to his mother. It is not enough that *she knows anyway*; it is crucial that he *tell* her explicitly, "Mom, I am gay." The actual conveying of information is of secondary importance; chances are, she *does* already know—on some level. The primary reason for the gay son to come out is for him to be able to address his own internalized homophobia. That can best be accomplished by giving a voice to his truth.

Furthermore, if he conceals his sexuality, he colludes with his mother in the fantasy by giving the impression that he really is someone else—*not* a queer. And he can further collude in the fantasy by believing that such information, if revealed, could cause harm. How can we harm people by telling them who we are? The gay man, struggling to find his Warrior, can no longer emotionally afford to agree to such terms. When a gay man comes out to his mother, the fantasy-lover relationship, which may have been developing over years, begins to disintegrate.

A former client, a 39-year-old gay man, whom we'll call Blake, just couldn't seem to figure out why he had never been able to find a lover. Quite strikingly handsome, Blake was an avid gardener, well read, articulate, with a wide-range of interests. He had a successful career and a beautiful home, which he had designed. Overall, he was a high-functioning person. Unfortunately, he had never been able to sustain a relationship for more than a few months. He was seeking therapy, desperately hoping to figure out this problem.

"Why can't I find a partner?" Blake would ask sadly. His dilemma over his single status had become an obsession. He shared, with a dejected tone, that he'd tried everything to find a man...running ads in the personals section of the local paper, searching the Internet, doing volunteer work at a local AIDS organization. Nothing seemed to work for him.

Finally, after several months of therapy and a fair amount of resistance in discussing his relationship with his mother ("What does *she* have to do with it, anyway?"), he agreed to explore that realm. Blake's parents had divorced when he was a child, and although his mother had remarried twice, her last relationship had ended in divorce ten years earlier. Since that time she had lived by herself and had no family other than Blake. Blake described his relationship with his mother as very loving and added that "maybe we're a little too close." He realized she relied heavily on him to satisfy her needs for emotional intimacy. He described how they would have lengthy conversations over the phone several times a week. In these conversations, she would confide in him about her personal life. Blake would listen compassionately and comfort her when she became lonely. When it was his turn, he would talk about his work or his house, but would intentionally veer away from any discussion about relationships or other personal matters.

Blake eventually disclosed in therapy that he had never come out to his mother. He shared this information in a casual tone, almost skipping over it, as though it were as incidental as what he had eaten for lunch. When asked why he withheld such information from her, he became somewhat anxious, saying he knew if he came out to her, "It would just kill her, and besides, she probably knows anyway."

Blake had successfully convinced himself that it was the fear of something awful happening to his mother that kept him in a place of secrecy. However, he was splitting off a huge piece of his identity. He believed, at least consciously, that he was hiding his sexuality from his mother in an attempt to protect her. (Any time we're trying to protect someone from our truth, we need to closely examine our real motives.)

Blake's unconscious motive to stay in hiding was an attempt to protect himself. "Oh, well, I'm sure she *knows*," he insisted. "I just don't see any reason to talk about it and upset her." As the work continued, it became apparent that Blake did, in fact, have a partner. It was his mother—Violet.

His mother probably *did* know Blake was gay, and she probably *had* known it for a long time. Most mothers seem to have a strong intuitive ability concerning such matters. The point is not whether they know it. The point is that we must tell them, not for their sake, but for ours. If we don't tell them about our sexuality, then we can't talk about our gayness, i.e., our essence. And that which we can't talk about, diminishes our power. Our power comes from who we are, not from who we pretend to be.

Whatever personal qualities we withhold, we are diminished proportionately. If we can't talk about any and all aspects of ourselves with the people we care about, then we won't be whole, vibrant, strong gay men. Instead, we become one-dimensional, asexual stick figures, only talking about certain "safe" issues, censoring huge areas of our daily existence in the name of self-protection.

Gay men can become emotionally castrated as long they agree to be in collusion with their mothers—that is, in agreeing to participate in the lie by keeping their gayness a secret from them. What's more, as long as a mother can perceive her son as a kind of sexless being, she can stay in denial and maintain the fantasy that she is her son's lover. The likelihood of such a fantasy increases if she's had an emotionally unavailable husband, as so many of our fathers have tended to be. If so, there's a good chance that she, knowingly or otherwise, has sculpted her son into her surrogate husband.

This experience is certainly not confined to gay men. As Sam Keen explains, "As a friend told me: 'Mother made me into the husband my father never was. I was the listener, the helper, the ally in hard times. In a sense I became the man of the house. I was superresponsible [sic], so I never really got a chance to be a kid'" (Keen, p.20). When there is a gay child around, a mother will, quite often, choose *him* as her confidant and substitute husband.

The moment a son reveals his gayness, the mother is forced to begin perceiving him in a new way—as a viable, sexual being, whose love object is male-specific—which excludes her. Faced with that realization, there is much less chance for her to sustain the fantasy.

As long as Blake stayed in hiding, his mother could stay in denial, holding on to a false perception of her son. She could maintain, albeit unconsciously, the fantasy that Blake would continue to be her surrogate husband. Blake's choice, not to come out to his mother, was keeping him emotionally and psychically chained to her, and preventing him from finding a satisfying relationship with a man. By not coming out to her, and by remaining enmeshed and never learning to set appropriate boundaries, Blake had lost his power. He couldn't fully exercise his gayness, more than through brief encounters, because his sense of allegiance to his mother outweighed his need for genuine sexual intimacy and for a committed, sustainable, long-term relationship with another man.

Additionally, the Violet and Sebastian syndrome exists when a gay son allows his mother to become overly involved in his life, and thus is unable to establish and maintain appropriate boundaries with her. In the case of Blake, his mother was using him as an emotional confidant by sharing personal details of her life. Did she really need to be telling *him* these things? His mother's boundaries were often unclear, and for Blake, it was sometimes hard to know where his mother ended and where he began.

This lack of boundaries, while not necessarily overtly incestuous, is certainly *emotionally* incestuous and can become very uncomfortable for the son. Without a clearer sense of boundaries or delineation between self and mother, it is hard for a gay man to be in touch with his Warrior.

■   ■   ■

As Robert Bly clearly points out in his analysis of the myth of *Iron John*, for a boy to move from a place of innocence and naiveté to the place of a fully-functioning, "initiated" adult male, he must unlock the cage where Iron John has been imprisoned. In other words, he must discover the place where his deep, inner masculine resides. He must move from the realm of the mother to that of the father.

In order to accomplish this task, he must find the key to the cage. The key represents the boy's personal power, the power that the boy must use to tap into this inner masculine, what we call the Warrior. No male, gay or straight, can remain a child once he agrees to accompany Iron John. By definition, the *adult* male is no longer "Mama's little boy."

According to Bly, the sixties created the "soft male." This male was more sensitive to women's needs, he cried more easily and he was, overall, more in touch with his emotions. Although many men *and* women believed that this was what men needed, it was not the end of the journey. It was an important advancement, but men needed to take another step. They needed to get in touch with their "deep masculine."

This level of masculinity should not be confused with patriarchal power; rather it is the place where the "masculine soul" resides, and it is neither gay nor straight. This next step incorporates the soft male *with* the Warrior. In this area, we gay men are one step ahead of our straight brothers. We found the soft male in ourselves long ago and *now* must find the Warrior.

In the myth, the key to the inner masculine is, of course, located under the mother's pillow—and this is by no accident. As little boys, we handed over our power, the key to our masculinity, to our mothers. Now, in order to reclaim that power, we have to get the key. (Dad could help us, but he's usually not available.) And we can't wait for Mom to return it. We have to steal it. A mother, unless she understands the importance of helping her son reclaim his power, is not usually willing to give it back. She's not going to walk up to the son one day and say, "Here's the key that was entrusted to me so long ago. It represents your personal power and is the path to your deep masculine, your warrior, and I want you to have it back."

"A mother's job is, after all, to civilize the boy, and so it is natural for her to keep the key" (Bly, p. 11). She's especially not going to give it back if her emotional needs are not getting met from other men in her world, namely her husband. If her gay son is her main source of emotional intimacy, chances are she's going to try to hold on to that connection, to the key, with tenacity because on some level she may know that our reclaiming the key means the end of the fantasy. "Mothers are intuitively aware of what would happen if he got the key: they would lose their boys. The possessiveness that mothers typically exercise on sons…can never be underestimated" (Bly, p. 12).

Von Franz explains:

> …masculine spontaneity is what the mother who intends to keep, or destroy, her son, instinctively fights. [She fights] the little **man** in the boy, which must be crushed at once. She hates [the feeling of masculine vitality] in the son because that is the impulse of life which will lead him away from her… (p.127-128).

One of the best ways to determine how much of the key Mom still has, is for the gay man to look at his behavior around her. Questions to consider are these:

- How old do I feel when I'm with my mother?
- What information do I share with her and why?
- How often do I talk to her?
- Does it ever feel excessive?
- Are there times when I shouldn't be telling her as much as I do about my personal life?
- Are there times when I shouldn't be listening to as much as I do about *her* personal life?
- Do I challenge my mother when there are apparent boundary violations between us?
- Do I tend to let these issues slide?
- Do I give her special treatment because "she's my mother?"

When a gay man is "in his Warrior," he can confront his mother on issues, share information with her that's appropriate, as well as not share information when he so chooses. He can feel his real age and can stay in that adult ego state throughout the duration of the interaction. In short, he has a sense of who he is, independent of who she is. This is how a gay man can feel and act *after* he has divorced his mother. It's what Initiation is all about.

Sheldon Kopp describes an example of his own struggle with his mother's attempt to keep the key from him in a case of symbolic castration when he was just past puberty:

My mother seemed especially disturbed by any sign of sexual maturity or independence. She would say things like: "Just because you've got hair on your chest doesn't mean you're a big shot." But clearly it was not the hair on my chest which most distressed her. She finally opted for splitting the difference with me by displacing the location of the crisis to the hair which had begun to grow under my arms.

She insisted that a "Big horse like you" should begin to use underarm deodorants. Then she began to nag that these deodorants would not be effective unless I shaved the hair under my arms as she did under hers. I still feel embarrassed to remember that I was at that time so much cast within the family scenario that I somehow went along with this symbolic ritual castration. At some point when my father was "on the road" she "helped" me with this problem.

Why is it so difficult for a mother to let her gay son reclaim his power? One, she may have a special connection with that gay son; he may be "her chosen one." Two, she may not want to give up her surrogate husband. Having a surrogate can seem a lot more attractive than no husband at all. Three, she may find the idea very threatening, unnecessary and/or just plain incomprehensible.

Even if the mother knows that she must let go of her son and give him over to the world of the father in order for him to grow into manhood, she has little support from society in helping her to do so. As well, she has a limited understanding of the concept of initiation. But most often, in all fairness to her, the mother simply doesn't realize the damage that is being done to her son in keeping him psychically tied to her. The idea of sending her son into the unknown world of men can be terrifying to her, especially when the father isn't there to greet the arriving boy. (The fact that fathers are often unwilling or incapable of taking over the care of the son is dealt with in the next chapter of this section). Therefore, mothers must be *taught* to let go and that is not an easy task!

As Blake continued his work, he began to see how his relationship with his mother was indeed affecting various areas of his life. Consequently, he started a process of emotional and psychic separation from her, a process of taking back the key. First he came out to her; and in time, he worked at setting healthier boundaries, such as being able to say "No" when he needed to. Blake was beginning a journey of initiation into true adulthood. He was learning how to divorce his mother, or at least that part of his mother that represented Violet.

Divorcing Violet is essential for all sons, but there are some specific reasons why it is particularly important for gay sons. A gay son's fight to reclaim his power from his mother, to divorce Violet, can be an even more arduous task than for straight sons. In general, mothers tend to align more closely with their gay sons. There are exceptions to this rule, certainly, but it's a pattern we observe in a high percentage of cases.

Maybe a mother finds in her gay son a heightened sensitivity, an ability not unlike her own, to use emotions as well as intuition to organize information and make sense of the world. Perhaps the behavioral and affective qualities that a gay son exhibits are part of a genetic code: in the DNA strands that the mother has passed on to him, qualities that she recognizes as being like her own. Whatever the reasons for this special connection that mothers and their gay sons seem to share, it presents, without question, certain liabilities in the their initiation process.

For the straight son, once he marries, he will be more apt to shift his allegiance from his mother to his wife. His wife, then, in certain important respects, replaces his mother as the primary woman in his life. (Unquestionably this shift does not always occur and the results can be equally as disastrous.)

Conversely, for the gay son, even if he has a partner, his mother can continue to remain his #1 woman. She faces no competition and thus can feel less need to relinquish her place of importance in her gay son's life. More importantly, the gay son may feel less need to shift his allegiance from his mother to his partner, and thus unconsciously remain in that fantasy love relationship with her.

In order for a healthy, intimate relationship to occur, the gay man *must*, at some point, transfer his allegiance from his mother to his partner. Otherwise, the continued, incestuous bond with his mother will undermine his chances of a relationship with *any* prospective partner.

For the gay man whose mother is already deceased, the work remains the same. In ways, the task of divorcing a mother who's already dead may be even more complicated, for only the image of mother remains. The son may have convinced himself that, because she is now gone, he has finally been able to "let go" of her. This is not necessarily so. Often, a gay man continues to show an unhealthy degree of loyalty to his mother long after her death; in some cases, that loyalty may even increase as he begins to idealize her and create a lofty, larger-than-life, albeit unrealistic, image. He must become aware of how he may be continuing to invest in the fantasy relationship. How he may be keeping his mother Violet—and remaining her Sebastian.

One of the main reasons that it is so hard for a gay man to divorce Mom is that often she was the *only* support he had growing up. Without his mother, where would he be and what would have happened to him? This is certainly a valid position that many men assume in defending their relationship with their mothers.

For many men, their fathers just weren't around, or they had no idea how to deal with their sons, or they had little interest. In his book *Uncharted Lives*, Stanley Siegel addresses the *pre-conscious* awareness of the gay child's world. Siegel maintains that everyone in the child's world, on a pre-conscious level, is aware of his sexuality. This is not a *conscious* awareness;

rather, it lurks just below the threshold of consciousness. As a result of this pre-conscious awareness, Dad, sensing the gay son's difference from his other children, may pull away even further from this particular child.

Even though the gay son wants his father's approval and love, more often than not, Dad is nowhere in sight. The child, struggling for survival, turns to what is often the only love available, his mother. Herein lies, perhaps, the genesis of the inordinately strong attachment between gay son and mother, and further illustrates the importance, and absolute necessity, of consciously breaking the emotional bond with the mother. Until we realize that we have our *own* power and that Mom can't give it to us, we remain children, incapable of healthy, adult relationships, *far removed from the powerful, Gay Warrior.*

Divorcing Violet does not mean that a gay man has to stop loving his mother. In fact, we are not speaking of love here at all, but rather, unhealthy allegiance. Certainly, he can continue to love this very important person in his life. But, (and this is a very important "but"), he must *change* his relationship to her. His very survival as a Warrior depends on it.

WHERE'S DAD?

How Our Fathers Betray Us

A friend told me, "My father was a traveling salesman, but even when he was at home he wasn't close to me. All my life I have suffered from uncertainties about my masculinity. I think it is because he never shared himself with me. He didn't tell me what kinds of problems he wrestled with, what he felt, what it meant to him to be a man. I have had to make it all up for myself, and I'm never sure that I have it right."
— *Fire in the Belly*, Sam Keen, p.137.

What undid them was their father's *silence*.
— *Stiffed*, Susan Faludi, p. 597.

A father most often betrays his gay son through emotional abandonment. There are two main reasons so many men of our father's generation have abandoned their sons. The first is historical and affects all sons—gay and straight—to varying degrees; the other is psychological and pertains specifically to gay men.

From an historical perspective, a father's emotional unavailability and subsequent abandonment of his son may be attributed to how men have been conditioned in the last 200 years—since the beginning of the Industrial Revolution. It is well documented by people like Robert Bly and James Hillman that the Industrial Revolution changed the man's relationship to himself and to his family, more than any other single event in our history. Not only did industry take men away from their homes and their families, it required them to work daily, every week of the year, with very minimal free time. The result was that for the first time in history men had very little time with their families, to know and be known by them.

Before the Industrial Revolution, fathers were able to spend more time with their sons, and from that time together, sons learned more directly from their fathers what it meant to be a man. As Bly explains, the boy learned about manhood from standing next to his father, shoulder to shoulder. Certain energy passed between father and son. The father didn't even have to talk; the boy learned from being with him. *When the father is not present, a son will have great difficulty in learning to become a man.*

In that time men experienced more continuous connection with their families and had more "down" time during certain seasons, which gave them more opportunity to be involved in the daily functioning of the family. When the Industrial Revolution began, sons, who had spent large amounts of time with their fathers learning their trade, working side by side with them in the shop or in the field, now were left in the care of their mothers. It was precisely at this point that the transfer of allegiance from mother to father, that a process of Initiation provides, ended. Metaphorically, and literally, the son had lost the father.

The Industrial Revolution not only took men away from their villages, but it also taught them not to feel. It's not that they were told "Don't Feel!"—it just happened as a part of the evolution of that age. In a collective sense, it was for the good of industry that men, inadvertently, learned such a lesson. For had they stayed in touch with their emotional bodies, they would have had to feel the sadness, the frustration and confusion of being separated from their families. Such an emotional state would have been counter-productive to the spirit of industry and progress.

Our fathers, as products of their age, were taught *en masse* to be disconnected from their feelings. From an early age, at home, in school and later in the work place, they learned not to feel, to place work above all other responsibilities, and to expect their wives to assume the bulk of the child-rearing duties. Their fathers before them were taught the same lessons. The consequence of this generational patterning is that we live in a society where fathers, for the most part, are disconnected from their emotional bodies and do not understand the importance of *being* with their sons, of talking to them, listening, and sharing with them their life experiences—their joys, sorrows and fears.

A more current historical factor that contributes to the emotional shut down that is present in so many fathers is their intense and unresolved grief from their war experience. The GI's who fought in WWII came home to a country that viewed them as heroes. They had won the war. But such adoration as was often showered on them easily mitigated their own sense of loss and grief for having had to kill—no matter how illustrious the cause.

As Faludi maintains, our fathers, the heroes of the "Great War", never successfully processed their grief, which would have included taking a close and painstaking look at their participation in killing other human beings and participating in other horrendous acts of war. Our fathers returned to an America that wanted them only to focus on their triumphal accomplishments. After all, they had successfully vanquished the Evil Empire and returned whole countries to free states. Even if they relived their war experiences, especially through reminiscing with "buddies", they usually did so under the guise of reinforcing their victor status and not to look at the shadow dimensions of war: the extinguishing of human life. "Postwar culture denied its returning soldiers the opportunity to grapple publicly with their horrific secret burden (not to mention the more public horrific burden of the war's atomic-bomb finale), thereby denying them a moral knowledge to pass down to the sons" (p. 378).

From a psychological perspective, a father's abandonment can be the result of his inability to come to terms with his gay son's differentness. The father might not be able to name that differentness; nevertheless, he has a feeling from the time his son is very young that there is something peculiar or odd about this child. This feeling can cause him to pull away from his gay son in subtle yet harmful ways. In his book, *Uncharted Lives, Understanding the Life Passages of Gay Men*, Stanley Siegel states, "...there exists evidence of a preconscious awareness of a different sexual orientation, both in the individual's mind and in the minds of older observers, members of the individual's family: parents, siblings, aunts, uncles, grandparents, and cousins" (p. 32).

Sadly, many fathers are ill equipped to deal with the specific needs of their gay sons, and in time, they abandon them. This abandonment can happen in both overt and subtle ways, and over time, creates in the son a sense of unworthiness, shame, and low self-esteem. When a father's own issues, his unhealed wounding, his past losses, his insecurities, possibly his own confusion over his sexuality get in the way, he then isn't able to be there for his gay son; he abandons his son. The son must then figure out his world by himself or create his own definition for what it means to be a man. Through this process, the gay son doesn't learn how to trust men or bond with them; instead, he may develop a deep and unconscious fear of later abandonment.

In his book, *Being Homosexual*, Dr. Richard Isay maintains that the relationship that a father has with his gay son, by its very nature, is often characterized by distance and uneasiness and is, therefore, fundamentally different from the relationship that the father might have with a straight son.

Isay describes the relationship between the father and the gay son from a psychoanalytic point of view, explaining the likelihood of the gay son developing an Oedipal complex, only in reverse. Instead of competing with his father for the love of his mother, the gay son unconsciously vies with his mother for his father's attention and approval. He unconsciously wishes to replace his mother, thereby becoming his father's central love object.

Isay theorizes that effeminate behavior in the young, gay boy is the attempt to mimic the mannerisms of his mother in order to win the affection of his father. He goes on to say that the father's level of homophobia (depending on the degree to which his feelings about his own masculinity remain unresolved or in question), may result in the father emotionally distancing himself from his gay son in a manner that he may not be inclined to do with a straight son. "Some of the fathers of homosexual boys either consciously or unconsciously recognize that their sons have both a special need for closeness and an erotic attachment to them" (p.34). Few fathers, however, are equipped to deal with such specific needs of a gay son.

> And some homosexual boys may sense in their fathers—especially those who cast an extremely heterosexual image—a rejection that they then intensify and internalize. Because the son feels he cannot be what his father wants, he seeks refuge in the understanding of a perhaps more sympathetic mother, who can temporarily shield her gay son from the disappointment and latent suspicions of his father. In other words, *homosexuality may actually cause a young boy to be distant from his father and close to his mother, rather than be caused by it.*" (Italics ours)
> — *Virtually Normal*, Andrew Sullivan, p. 10.

THE CONSEQUENCES OF ABANDONMENT

Since we didn't trust our fathers and they didn't trust us, it's difficult for us to trust any man fully. If you did not trust your father in general, then you can't trust him as a masculine role model. Consequently, you can't trust yourself and your masculinity...So if a man can't trust anyone with a cock to be caring, compassionate, and considerate, he looks toward the other gender for this emotional support, and for models of behavior.
— *At My Father's Wedding*, John Lee, p. 43.

A father's emotional unavailability and subsequent abandonment can have far-reaching and profound consequences for his gay son. Such consequences may include: difficulty trusting other men, a fear of abandonment, feeling unsafe in groups of men, a preference to find safety among women, a proclivity toward dishonesty, a tendency to seek out inappropriate surrogate fathers, and a damaged view of the archetypal father and of God.

Many gay men have difficulty trusting other men. In our work with gay men (in both individual and group therapy) one of the biggest problems discussed is lack of trust. Is it any wonder that gay men have difficulty trusting other men? Most of us learned from our most important male model not to trust. Let's take a closer look at this.

As children, the trust in our fathers diminished as the unspoken agreement between them and us was broken. This agreement would include: a father's responsibility to love and protect his son; to be there for him and to help him grow and support him in becoming whomever he's meant to become; to nurture him and to make the world a safe place for him; to tell him he is great and that he will love his son no matter who he is.

Chances are, very little of this kind of agreement did most of our fathers honor. So if the gay son never learned to genuinely trust his father, what does this mean for him later in life as a gay adolescent and adult? Clearly, this speaks to one of the gay man's greatest dilemmas. It is only a small step further to say that if a man doesn't trust his father; he won't trust other men.

The consequence for the son with an absentee father is that he doesn't learn to trust the most important man in his life. On a collective level, it points to why men don't trust other men. Certainly this fact is what fuels competition rather than cooperation. One must trust to cooperate. Even though this is true for straight men as well, the difference is straight men aren't seeking other men for partners. A gay man desires to be with a man, but how can he find one if he can't trust him?

If he never learned how to trust his father, the first man in his life, his first *sex-appropriate* love object, then how is he going to know how to trust other men? And if a gay man can't trust men, the segment of the population in which he looks for a potential partner, then how is he going to have a successful relationship? As well, how is the gay man going to form a positive view of his own masculinity, of the world of men, or of God? Herein lies the paradox: Gay men are sexually attracted to the very group of people that they may least trust. To better understand this paradox, it is essential that gay men recognize how their fathers may have impaired their ability to trust.

A gay man may prefer the company of women where he can feel more comfortable, and ultimately safer. Such women may include his mother or his "best friend"—someone he turns to when he is really having a hard time. Even if he does feel more comfortable in a *group* of men rather than a *group* of women, chances are he has actually trusted a woman (or a series of women) more than he has ever trusted a man.

This may be evidenced when examining a relationship with a female employer or other women in power. Possibly the gay man feels more comfortable with a female boss. This could suggest that he ultimately trusts women more and that he has more power with a female than with a male. He may even feel more at ease in a group situation when there are at least some women present. Although there is nothing wrong, *per se*, with feeling safer with women, it may cause a gay man inadvertently to stay separated from men by seeking out the safety and comfort (and familiarity) of women, rather than learning how to feel safe with men as well.

Group situations can often remind the gay man of similar situations in his youth when he was intimidated or abused by groups of boys. Whether this was intentional or not, he felt uncomfortable. There is little doubt that most gay boys had difficulties being in groups of other boys. The image of a young gay boy surrounded by a group of his girlfriends is a common occurrence. Many gay men report having had close girlfriends, but few boyfriends. On the other hand, straight boys would much rather be around groups of boys than girls. They may have a "girlfriend," but woe to the boy who wanted to hang out with the girls!

As a gay boy matures, his sexual desires focus more and more on other boys. But if he doesn't feel a sense of trust or safety around them, he will begin to feel a "cognitive dissonance"—that is, his mistrust will conflict with his desire. Later, when his desire for sex and relationships grows stronger, he might find himself even more conflicted and unable to get his needs met.

When a gay boy does not have the support of his father, he develops alternative coping strategies in order to survive. One is to get really good at lying. A gay boy knows that, in order to survive, he had better conceal his true identity. So he begins to lie about his different feelings and his perceptions of the world. He understands that he must do this or else he will not make it!

When we speak of *not making it,* we are talking about literal survival. A father holds his son's life in the palm of his hand. He is the arbiter of his son's existence. The father is god to a child. It is very important that we understand the impact of the god-like power that a father possesses. The noted Jungian analyst and author, Marion Woodman, explains that, from an archetypal perspective, the father represents God. She maintains that if a man never learns to trust his father, then he can't trust God. Additionally, in many religious traditions, God is defined as omnipotent, omniscient, and omnipresent. He knows everything, is everywhere, and is all-powerful. Such qualities a child projects on to his father (and his mother). The child's entire world is filtered through his parents.

What happens to the child whose father (God) doesn't want to spend time with him or disapproves of him? What does it mean when the most powerful man in the child's world does not show him that he is loved? Where does the child learn to trust that men will be there for him when he is in need? The answer is simple. He doesn't. He grows up and expects men to abandon him and more often than not, they do.

Most gay men did not receive adequate instruction from their fathers on how to become strong, healthy men, i.e. how to express emotions as a man, how to communicate as a man, how to work through conflict constructively. Consequently, they often defer to other men in positions of authority to emulate and to help them develop a sense of manhood. Sometimes these models are healthy; other times, not. If these men in places of power were taught the principles of Initiation, then they may serve as appropriate surrogate fathers. If they haven't done their own separation work, they're not going to be able to help others do theirs. With men who are not truly initiated, it is just a matter of time before *their Puer*, who is still running *their* show (and sometimes running *our show*) will be exposed.

How can a gay man learn about trust, safety, honesty and closeness if his father was not able to teach him? One way is by finding a mentor—an older man, a father substitute, who can help the young man make this shift of allegiance from the realm of the feminine to the masculine and thus move to a place of more genuine adulthood. A mentor relationship requires time, care and attention—factors not always readily available in today's world. Such a replacement father may come in a variety of forms—a teacher, a craftsman, an elder, or a therapist. In order for this mentor relationship to be successful, several key components must be present. One, the relationship should remain non-sexual. The moment it becomes sexual, it becomes a "peer" dynamic. Two, it must have a clearly-defined purpose that both mentor and protégé agree to. And three, it must include safety, trust, and honesty.

In the end, a big piece of a gay man's initiation work is in coming to terms with the ways in which his father fell short of providing him with adequate modeling of being a man. This would include feeling the grief of the father who never was. It means getting honest about how the father did not teach his son to feel good about his gayness; instead he never talked with him about his differentness (even though everyone in the family was probably aware of that differentness). And last, it means finding appropriate, alternative male models to offer support and guidance in his initiation process.

Such models may be available to a gay man in a variety of forms, including psychotherapy. At some point in a gay man's healing/recovery process, we believe it is essential that he work with a male therapist, and preferably a gay therapist. A gay therapist will have a visceral understanding of the issues that the client brings with him into the work. His knowledge of sexual orientation will come from an experiential place rather than a theoretical one. We will discuss this issue more in PART IV: A Contemporary Form of Initiation.

Even though both gay and straight men suffer in having fathers who are not there for them, it is quite possible that a father's emotional unavailability may have a more profound effect on the development of a gay son than a straight son. For the gay son, the father is his first same-sex love object. The gay son, from day one, will formulate a perspective of what men are like based on his observations of his father's actions and interactions (or lack of) with him. That perspective will serve as the basis for his understanding of what an appropriate love object will look like in years to come, and he will undoubtedly try to create intimate relationships based on such a perspective. Conversely, for the straight son, it is his mother who serves as the primary model for the young boy's developing sense of romantic love. That is, a straight son's primary love object is the mother.

In our work with gay men who have straight brothers, they will often speak of the acceptance that their brothers received from their fathers. In reality, their brothers probably received very little more from them; but nevertheless, there seems to be an understanding between fathers and straight sons. They intuitively view the world in a similar way. From this perspective, it makes sense that many gay men couldn't connect with their fathers—even for those with fathers who, given a chance, would have wanted more connection. These men didn't have the slightest idea how to go about relating to their gay sons or in working through the psychological challenges that such a relationship presented.

A FATHER'S ABUSE

A client, whom we'll call Sam, came into therapy to work on relationship difficulties. He had had a string of short-lived experiences, but invariably his partner turned out to be "the wrong man." When asked about his relationship with his father, Sam described it as having been "pretty bad" early on, but added that he and his father had later reached an "understanding." When asked to elaborate on what kind of understanding they had, Sam explained that his father had stopped picking on him for being gay, and that he no longer humiliated him for his effeminate behavior. In giving an example of what picking on him looked like, he recounted the following story. Most readers would find this story overtly abusive, but to Sam these were just his "normal" childhood memories.

One time when Sam was twelve, his father caught him trying on an older sister's dress. Flying into a rage, his father threw Sam out of the house and forced him to stand in the front yard for over an hour so that the neighbors could see how "ridiculous" he looked. This memory was etched in his mind. Never had he been able to get over the shame and sense of powerlessness that he felt. But he didn't consider what his father had done as abusive. Rather, as he explained, "It was just the way he showed his concern for me. He didn't want me to be gay and this was his way of dealing with it." In Sam's mind, Dad's abuse had been transformed into Dad's concern.

Not surprisingly, Sam tended to seek out men who would abuse him—both physically and verbally. He had developed a love frequency, based on Dad's behavior that coupled abuse with care, thereby seeking out men who carried a similar energetic frequency to that of his father's.

Unfortunately Sam's father continued to abuse him. In a recent phone conversation, his father had told him that, "...all queers end up dying of AIDS. And if you get sick, don't expect your mother and me to take care of you." But despite this blatant and highly toxic abuse, Sam felt he had a duty to call and visit this man regularly.

He, like most adult sons, wanted his father to love and approve of him. Even though his father continued to demonstrate, through consistent and repeated actions, that he did not love or approve of him, Sam kept going back for more. Up to that point, Sam had been willing to do just about anything to obtain his father's love, including sacrificing his self worth.

After more than a year in therapy, Sam came to his session one day and presented in a restless manner. He was clearly upset, but didn't know how to begin. "My dad doesn't love me," he finally said reluctantly. "He has never loved me." Tears began to roll down Sam's cheeks. Then, as if some inner emotional damn was cracking open, he began to sob. Although in great pain, Sam had just turned an important emotional corner. This insight indicated that Sam's long-held and very faulty belief—namely that abuse=love—was beginning to collapse. He realized that his father's abusive treatment was *just* that—abuse.

Sam was on the threshold of shifting to a new energetic frequency, one that could be based on authentic love rather than on fantasy. In order for him to see what love was, he had to understand what it was not. For the first time, he was willing to consider that what he had been receiving from his father all his life, and had unconsciously mistaken for love, wasn't about love at all. Sam was beginning to find his way out of the emotional labyrinth that had held him prisoner. It would take several more years of therapy for Sam to create a new understanding of what love *could* be, but he was now on his way.

Sam's process is a classic example of Initiation. In coming to terms with the reality that his father did not love him, he was able to shatter the fantasy that had kept him in a relationship limbo, where he never found what he was looking for.

To acknowledge that one has not been loved, especially by a parent, takes tremendous courage. It also requires the faith that such knowledge will not destroy the individual, but rather help him become a more integrated/initiated adult. When this is the case, it is an adult function to look at one's life honestly enough to admit, "Perhaps my parent(s) did not love me." It goes without saying that if one's parents were truly loving, then this particular process is unnecessary. But all too often, especially for the gay man, one or both parents may not have been able to truly love him. *And if this is the case*, it is imperative that he come to terms with this truth. His very survival depends on it.

Although Sam's story seems like an extreme one, it is not. Abuse comes in many different shapes and sizes, and is not always so overt as in the case of this client. Often it is more subtle or covert. It may be a nonverbal disdain that the parent carries for his gay child. However the delivery, whether verbal or non-verbal, whether overt or subtle, if the message that the parent is sending is: *I do not accept you for who you are*, this is abuse.

We must begin to understand that when people abuse us, *they are not loving us.* Until we really understand this, we will continue to mistake the abuse frequency for love. So long as we couple abuse with love, we are lost. To undo this faulty perception of love, we have to be able to say no to the abuse. Saying no might mean confronting the abuser. In extreme cases, it might mean having to walk away from the relationship, knowing that we are doing so for our highest good.

As children, if our parents abused us, we were defenseless against that abuse. We were victims. True victims do not have a choice. They are powerless over their abuser. As adults, barring extreme circumstances (such as random violence or war), we always have a choice to stop abuse. Adults who allow themselves to be abused (in this case by parents) are continuing to agree to an old emotional "contract" that says: *abuse is acceptable.* Even if this contract seems real, it is only a perception and perceptions can be changed. Often it is frightening to let go of old ways of dealing with the world, including the contracts that we may have made with a parent long ago.

In *A Little Book on the Human Shadow*, Bly explains that "every act of cruelty, conscious or unconscious, that our parents take, we interpret as an act of love." This interpretation occurs because of the power of the fantasy bond. Then, when you become an adult, cruelty and love will be mixed together. Every time someone does something cruel to you, you will image that there is some love in it. This can keep someone stuck in an abusive relationship forever. Every bit of love that you feel from others, you will long for some cruelty in it. Furthermore, there will always be some cruelty in the love you feel for others.

For Sam, allowing his dad to abuse him was a pattern of relationship he was very familiar with. People often opt to stay in old patterns, however destructive, because they are familiar. The alternative, to try something different, might be too frightening. Human beings seem to have a proclivity for choosing what they know, over what's in their best interest. In staying in an old pattern, we know what to expect; by trying something different, we may have to venture into the unknown.

Some parents know how to love their children; many do not. This is an issue that is not being talked about enough. If all parents truly knew how to love their children, the world would not be in such a sad state. Our definition of love, whether positive or negative, originates with our parents.

When authentic love exists, a child forms a healthy view of himself and his world. He understands his place in the world; he feels a sense of safety and trust and knows that he is cared for.

When a child is not loved, he will nevertheless fantasize that he *is* loved. Robert Firestone calls this the fantasy bond. It is too painful for a child to consciously acknowledge that a parent does not love him; such awareness would threaten his existence. As explained before, parents represent God to a child. What does it mean when God does not love him? This is too devastating to a child, so the child develops a relationship with the parent in his fantasy. *Daddy really loves me; he's just busy. Daddy didn't really mean those things he said; he's just tired. My father loves me; it's just in his own way.*

Furthermore, because the child cannot acknowledge parental weakness and must maintain the idealized image of the parent as good and powerful, the child develops a negative self image and sees himself as bad. The child must perceive himself as "bad, unlovable, and undeserving. The child must interpret parental rejection as being his or her fault since the child needs to perceive the parents as being loving, competent people…These negative attitudes toward self become a prominent part of the self-concept and are at the center of the individual's self-hatred." (p. 79)

As long as a person clings to these beliefs, when they are not true, he is in trouble. When our parents really don't love us, and such a reality is more common than most people are willing to admit, we must get honest about it. If we don't, we are stuck with a very distorted definition of love. Certainly, coming to terms with not having been loved by a parent is the most difficult of psychological tasks, but if it is our experience, we must do so.

INITIATION AND THE FATHER

When a son metaphorically kills his father, he will have more energy. He'll get more things done than he would have if Dad's voice had been pushing him in other directions. He'd be more likely to act on Joseph Campbell's injunction, "Follow your bliss." He'd take back the projection of godliness he'd placed on his father, see him as "simply" human, and become more human himself. He'd stop making other men and women into the parent who wasn't there for him. He'd become an anchor to his own children and a model for masculinity and an adult when he's with his lover or wife. *The son who kills the father becomes a man and stops being a boy.* [italics ours]
— *At My Father's Wedding*, John Lee, p. 19.

One of the main purposes of Initiation is to help a boy—whether gay or straight—shift his allegiance from the world of the feminine to the masculine. It is very important to understand that this is a process exclusive to males. Since all children come from the mother, it is understandable that they all, under normal developmental circumstances, form a close attachment to her. The child is dependent on the mother for his/her very survival—usually more so than on the father.

For the young girl, it is her mother who will continue to serve as her primary model for her developing sense of femininity. A daughter watches her mother move through her world, and in so doing, she learns how women express their emotions, how they relate to men, how they dress, their values, their attitudes. For the young boy, just the opposite is true.

As a boy grows older, his needs expand beyond basic survival and, in time, he will need to have a solid model for what it means to be a man. At some point the son must separate from his mother, in order to learn these lessons. For this his mother cannot help him, however hard she may try. For healthy development of masculinity to occur, the boy must, at some point, break from the world of his mother and begin to immerse himself more fully in the world of his father. We're speaking here more in theoretical terms, painfully aware that such a shift seldom occurs —particularly for the gay child. However, an examination of this shift is necessary so that we may begin to find the missing pieces of the puzzle, and so we may develop alternative ways of completing this developmental passage. One thing is certain; no one can make this shift without assistance.

In our culture most boys—gay or straight—do not experience this shift, and often stay unhealthily attached to the mother. Indigenous cultures recognized this long ago and so built initiation rituals that incorporated large numbers of the community to assist the boy in his process. Within that context, the boy was able to use his father as a model for learning how men expressed their emotions, what their values and attitudes were, and how they related to other men and to women. In general, the boy learned, by watching his father move through his world, what it meant to be a man.

If the father is not around—physically and/or emotionally—and if the boy does not have substitute male models, he will not receive this fundamental instruction. If he does not receive such information, he will be more inclined to stay unhealthily connected indefinitely to his mother in an attempt to find that missing piece of his masculinity that has continued to elude him.

In indigenous cultures, this shift from the feminine to the masculine is an integral component of Initiation. It begins in early adolescence when the young boy is removed from the safety and comfort of his mother's world and taken by the older men of the tribe to learn about the world of the masculine. He learns about the power of male nurturing or what Bly calls "male mothering."

Within the Pueblo tradition of the Native American people, a boy who is being initiated, enters a kiva where he learns the traditions, stories, dances, rituals and history of the tribe—all taught to him by the older men. Although the actual Initiation is left to the other men of the tribe, the father participates indirectly. He understands the value of the Initiation and supports the process. It is understood that the father is too involved in the situation to respond objectively, so the other men step in to help the young boy through this transitional time.

Since most of us never learned to make this shift from our mothers to our fathers, it becomes more and more clear as to where most of us gay men began to get stuck. Not only did most of our fathers abdicate the responsibility of parenting to our mothers, their lack of involvement in our lives had specific consequences for our developing sexual orientation.

We never learned how to trust, feel safe or develop intimacy with the group in which we would eventually seek out partnership. Today, we are often left adrift on the stormy sea of masculinity without map, compass, or rudder. We may inadvertently look for mentorship in older men, but until we identify what we're actually looking for, we may not fully take advantage of the guidance these men have to offer us. Additionally, we may send them mixed messages as to what we are really wanting from them.

When the father does not actively teach his son, gay or straight, how to be a man, the boy has no choice but to continue to learn about the world from his mother. He may develop a belief system based on feminine principles, form perceptions of men based on his mother's opinions of them, and learn to feel as a woman feels. Worst of all, he may even learn how to *be* a man from his mother.

Many of us gay men, when we were young, spent a lot more time with our mothers than with our fathers. (This is changing somewhat today as more fathers participate in the parenting of their children.) But for the majority of gay men who grew up pre-80's, they were probably more involved with their mothers. The problem here is not the amount of time the gay boy received from his mother; but rather the amount of time he didn't get to spend with his father.

A father's effectiveness as a parent can be largely assessed on the basis of his own level of Initiation. Since most fathers in our culture are uninitiated men, we sons have not learned from them how to make this shift of psychological and emotional allegiance from the world of the feminine to the masculine. If our fathers never learned how to healthily separate from their parents, it will be impossible for them to transmit to their sons a set of principles that they never learned.

The closest many of our fathers may have come to their own Initiation was through having been in the service. Many veterans look at their war experiences as the time in life when they felt most alive, most connected. But, as we have mentioned, just being a soldier does not automatically make a man a Warrior. If he has not also done the separation work from his family of origin, and grieved the shadow aspects of war (no matter how illustrious the cause), there will be vestiges of the *Puer* that he will continue to play out.

As with so many men of our fathers' generation, when the war ended, so did their aliveness. True Initiation would have allowed these men to continue, long after the war, to feel that level of passion, commitment, emotional intensity and love for something else—*such as their families.* If our fathers are not initiated men, they are not going to be able to help us become initiated.

The most pronounced feature of an uninitiated father is his inability to help his own son separate from him. If a father did not learn how to separate successfully from his mother and father, he will not know how to teach his son about Initiation, nor will he have the intellectual, emotional or spiritual understanding of why such a process is even necessary. A father's presence and participation (or lack thereof) in his gay son's Initiation greatly influences his son's perceptions of his own masculinity, and his eventual ability or inability to become a strong, self-actualized man. Let's consider for a moment what it would look like for a father to actually participate in his son's Initiation.

The initiated father helps initiate his son by demonstrating the following:

1) Knowing the appropriate time for his son to begin the process of Initiation.
2) Explaining to his son the importance of why he needs to separate from him and the rest of the family.
3) Actively participating in the process through conversations and/or ritual experience.
4) Allowing himself to grieve the loss of his son as his son, thus setting him free to become his own person with his own thoughts, values and sense of self, separate from his father and the rest of the family.
5) Knowing that helping his son to healthily separate is never about abandoning him.
6) Demonstrating his trustworthiness through actions and behaviors.
7) Modeling honesty.
8) Expressing a genuine sense of respect and love for his son.

When fathers are able to do this well, their sons can become adults. They will be in touch with their true masculinity and more able to connect with their world in a healthy way.

For the gay man to become a Warrior, he must also look closely at his relationship to his father. In doing so, he has one of two choices: He may view this relationship through the lens of the *Puer* that will tend to distort and, in many cases, idealize his father. Or he may see it though the eyes of the strong adult—the Warrior—who will be able to see with clarity and truth.

Whether he realizes it or not, this relationship has served as the primary model for how he views himself as a man, and about his understanding of love, trust, safety and intimacy with other men. What a gay man may often look for in a partner, consciously or otherwise, will be directly related to what he experienced early on with his father. If he experienced acceptance and trust, he will most likely seek out a partner who will show acceptance and trust. If he experienced rejection and/or abandonment from his father, he will often look for men who will disapprove of him and eventually leave him.

In her book *Stiffed: The Betrayal of the American Man*, Susan Faludi concludes that the most significant loss that we American men have suffered is the absence of our fathers and the ultimate abandonment by them. Whether gay or straight, most of us have been emotionally and psychologically "stiffed" by our fathers—men who were deeply shaped by the war (both WWII and the Korean War) and subsequent postwar work environments. American culture of the 40's stressed duty to country; in the 50's and 60's it stressed duty to work.

War taught our fathers to disconnect from their emotional experience. When they returned home, this was reinforced in the emerging corporate structure. Subsequently these men were unable to provide us with what we needed to figure out how to be strong, healthy, caring, conscious men. All too often, we were left to our own devices to try to find our way through the labyrinth of masculinity-formation. For most of us, we found ourselves walking in circles with a nagging sense that we would never find our way "out" and into the realm of true manhood.

PART III

HOW WE BETRAY OURSELVES

Of all the betrayals that a gay man suffers, perhaps the most poignant of all is the betrayal of self. No example of this is more striking than when he remains committed to his *Puer*, that archetypal force which will prevent him from ever becoming a powerful man—the Warrior.

To better understand the nature of the *Puer*, we have presented the most common patterns of this archetype found within the gay men we've worked with. These patterns include behaviors, perceptions, beliefs, and attitudes of the *Puer*. This exploration is intended to help gay men identify how this archetypal force is still in control, and to understand how the *Puer* adversely affects their daily lives. Such a task can only be accomplished by taking a close and painstaking look at how these patterns can keep us stuck, disempowered and isolated—the worst consequences of remaining little boys.

- The Good Boy
- The Narcissist
- The Addict
- The Irresponsible Boy
- The Oppressor

Within each of us gay men can be found varying degrees of some, if not all, of these patterns. Some patterns may appear to be more "positive" than others, but don't be fooled. All of them, however seemingly benign, are dangerous in a gay man's life. Until he is able to identify which particular *Puer* pattern(s) most often control his life, he will be unable to live as a mature, initiated man. Some men will identify most strongly with one of the patterns; others may relate to aspects of many or all of them. Whichever pattern(s) a gay man most strongly identifies with, should be the indicator of how his allegiance to the *Puer* plays out, and thus how he is most stuck in this archetypal energy.

> **Note:** Our intention in identifying the major *Puer* patterns is not to over-pathologize gay men, but rather to bring into focus that which keeps many men boy-like and disempowered. Certainly we all have many positive qualities that add to our uniqueness and beauty, but it is not the positive qualities that get in our way.

In PART IV, Transforming Betrayal Into Wisdom, we will discuss how the gay man can replace these *Puer* patterns with ones that will help him lead a richer, more productive and authentic adult life. This process is what we refer to as Initiation, the growing out of the *Puer*, whereby the gay man moves out of his adolescence and into true adulthood. For now, let's take a closer look at each of these *Puer* patterns.

THE GOOD BOY

I was a goody-goody because it was the proven road to reward.
It was the way to play the game.
Deep down, I knew I wasn't "good" at all—just selfish, just out for myself.
I was a phony, and I knew it.
　　from *The Best Little Boy in the World*, John Reid, p. 9.

The Good Boy is arguably the most visible part of a gay man's *Puer,* most likely because it was one of the main survival strategies that many of us learned early on in order to cope with an unsafe world. In a family environment that could range anywhere from non-supportive of our differentness, all the way to overtly homophobic, we quickly caught on to what was necessary for basic survival. That is, most of us had to learn from a very young age what we had to do to *literally* stay alive, to avoid being annihilated by our world. Often what we chose—consciously or other-wise—was to become exceptionally good.

The Good Boy does what people tell him to do, thinks the way others want him to think. He follows the rules and acts obediently. He goes to great lengths to get people to like him—by being nice, polite, compliant, docile and well behaved. He often uses humor to ingratiate himself to others. He strives to please. Whenever possible, he will smooth out the rough edges, act as a peacemaker, fence-mender, intermediary. And never does he make waves or rock the boat. In short, the Good Boy makes a great student council president.

Learning to be a Good Boy is the *Puer's* way of opting for survival over extinction. However, as John Reid points out in his funny (at times, painfully so) and poignant autobiography, *The Best Little Boy in the World*, the genesis of the Good Boy has very little to do with a belief that one is actually good. Instead, because the gay boy rarely, if ever, receives any acknowledgment or validation for his differentness, he concludes that who he is and how he feels is *not* good. Being a Good Boy is not so much about truly believing in one's goodness, as it is a psychological defense against an underlying belief of being intrinsically bad—unworthy, flawed, wrong.

Such an adaptive strategy, however understandable, carries a hefty price, especially when such behavior and thinking continue into adulthood. As with many defense mechanisms, those that served us well as children eventually begin to work against us as adults. Remaining a Good Boy long after childhood and adolescence prevents the gay man from ever finding his power. As Marie-Louise von Franz explains, "the puer aeternus…very often tends to be too impressed, too weak, and too much of a 'good boy' in his relationships, without a quick self-defense reaction [anger] where required" (p.47). When the gay man continues to play out the role of Good Boy, he will be a person without substance, who allows his world to treat him as someone who is insignificant and inconsequential.

CHARACTERISTICS OF THE GOOD BOY

The Good Boy embodies all of the so-called "positive" characteristics of the *Puer*:

- Avoidance of anger
- Lack of righteous indignation
- Premature forgiveness
- Intense and inappropriate emotional connection to parents
- Obedience/Following rules

Avoidance of Anger:

One of the quintessential features of the Good Boy is his avoidance of anger. As a gay boy learns to adapt to his environment, he will often avoid getting angry as a way of not calling attention to himself. *He who makes no waves is often left unseen, unheard.* For the gay boy who already feels tenuous and unsafe in his world, such a proposition can seem like the best of all solutions. Even though he will have ample reason to be angry—being the butt of homophobia; forever harassed by peers; called sissy, faggot, homo, pansy; and treated as an outcast at school, at home and in the community—he will learn early on to suppress his anger.

Many gay men, if they were conditioned to be Good Boys, never learned that anger expression is not only healthy but absolutely necessary in order to protect themselves from abuse, homophobia, and other types of oppression. Expressing anger, when done appropriately, is about defining and defending one's boundaries. John Bradshaw explains that anger protects our dignity; it tells us when our needs are not getting met.

When a gay man remains a Good Boy, he is cut off from his power source. He won't have a clue how to protect himself since he's never learned the value of anger. He will be what von Franz describes as "the yielding good boy"—pliable, ever-changing to fit the circumstance, always ready to please, unable to hold firm to a position. As well, he is what Robert Bly refers to as the "soft male"; he is the antithesis of Iron John, the deep masculine within that contains his power.

Lack of Righteous Indignation:

Since the Good Boy has often spent a lifetime avoiding and suppressing his anger, he will lack the ability to express righteous indignation. Righteous indignation, by its very definition, requires being oppositional when the situation warrants it. This is a task next to impossible for the Good Boy. Invested in being nice and compliant, the Good Boy accepts society's view of him as inconsequential and subordinate, and he will therefore lack the ability to know how and when to say "Enough."

The powerful adult gay man allows himself to feel his righteous indignation and express it. Examples would include actively confronting discrimination, prejudice, homophobia/homohatred in his world—his family, people at work, those in his community or political leaders. When he becomes the target of injustice, he is able to say, "How dare anyone try to deny me my basic human rights!" or "How dare the Religious Right tell me my sexuality is an abomination!"

Righteous indignation means not letting people in our world control and manipulate us with their homophobic agendas—conscious or otherwise. It means saying to them, "Your bigotry is unacceptable and I will not tolerate it one minute longer!" The moment we gay men find our righteous indignation, we stop being Good Boys, nice and proper and well behaved. In that moment, when we begin to embrace our power, we become a force to be reckoned with; something that much of our world might not want us to become.

Premature Forgiveness:

The Good Boy often wants to forgive, prematurely, the people in his world who have hurt and/or betrayed him (most specifically his parents and the other "main players" in his life). He may try to forgive too soon by denying the depth of his feelings or by trying to convince himself that he has somehow been able—as if through osmosis—*to just let go of all the hurt*. If he believes that forgiveness can be found without first working through all the feelings—especially the anger, the sadness and the mistrust—he will be seriously deceiving himself.

Before any of us can find true forgiveness, we need to let ourselves feel the full breadth of emotions related to the hurt. Next we need to direct those feelings at the appropriate target(s)—whether done actually or symbolically, (e.g. role-playing the situation in a therapy session). It is only through an active process that we can move through these feelings and be "finished" with them. In the case of severe abuse, it may take a long time to process all the feelings—especially the anger. Nevertheless, if a person is actively working through the anger, he will eventually finish with these pent-up emotions and move on with life. Regardless of what some people in the psychological community say, only when he is finished with his anger, can a person truly and honestly forgive—*and not one moment before.*

The Good Boy often uses a type of denial when he engages in premature forgiveness. A good example of such thinking was seen in a former client named Rick. When Rick came out to his parents at 15, his father, an active alcoholic full of rage and homophobia, threw him out. Rick, now 32, had only seen his father several times since for brief visits, and he described their relationship as "marginal." When asked how he felt about his father's overt rejection of his gayness, he stated that he held "no resentment toward the man." When asked how he had worked through his feelings toward a father who had so blatantly abused him, Rick's response was, "I decided a long time ago that he wasn't worth my anger, and so I just let go of it."

When pressed further as to where the anger had gone, he began to realize that he had buried it somewhere deep inside himself, and had only fooled himself into believing he had gotten rid of it. What he had failed to understand was that his anger had not just disappeared. Instead, it had remained deeply buried, causing some severe physical problems. His anger was eating away at him in the form of a stomach ulcer.

Many religions and new age philosophers encourage people to move directly into forgiveness by offering the pat answer: *Just do it!* In one of her tapes, Caroline Myss maintains that all someone has to do in order to forgive "…is just decide to do it". We could not disagree more. Forgiveness does not just happen. We have to do a lot of work first for it to even become a possibility. Myss' position reinforces the notion that forgiveness can happen magically, effortlessly and without any sort of process. It is unconscionable for religions or anyone else to tell us that we should simply "Turn the other cheek" or "Forgive thy neighbor" if they don't also teach us *how* to do it.

John Bradshaw believes that if nothing happened then there's nothing to be angry about. In other words, something must have happened to make us feel angry/ betrayed/untrusting. The path to forgiveness is through the process of actively expressing the feelings—not bypassing them.

Scott Peck explains, "Real forgiveness is a tough, tough process, but it is an absolutely necessary one for your mental health." The only way for a person to truly forgive his neighbor is to allow himself his anger. He must express his anger, and when possible, express it directly to the persons who deserve that anger. It's not going to kill them—*it's only anger!* It is important to note here that anger is not the same as rage. Rage is a completely different feeling. Healthy anger is proportional to the offense. Rage is completely disproportional; it always comes with past baggage.

Intense and Inappropriate Emotional Connection with Parents:
The Good Boy maintains an intense and inappropriate emotional connection to his parents. Examples of this would include his deferring to them when making important decisions, sharing too much of his personal life, or counting on them to bail him out if he gets in a jam. As we will explain in more detail in PART IV: "Leaving Home," what keeps a gay man most disempowered and boy-like is his abiding and unconscious allegiance to Mom and Dad.

Often a gay man's unhealthy emotional connection will play out most specifically with his mother. Here's one such example. Sam called his mother several times a week, and every time he and his lover had a fight, he was on the phone again. Sam's mother hated to see her son unhappy and gave advice that was not necessarily good for his relationship. Sam could not understand why his partner resented this, nor could he see how this was adversely affecting their relationship. What his behavior actually indicated was that his primary allegiance was to his mother.

In many primitive societies, this emotional bond is severed through rites of passage, or Initiation. In our society we must do the work without much support from our culture *or* our parents. Outwardly, society claims that breaking the emotional bonds with our family is a necessary step to adulthood, and stresses that it takes place in many ways, but the reality is quite the opposite. In fact, our society offers the gay man very few initiative opportunities and those that are available do not adequately accomplish the task. In order to become a mature adult, the gay man must break his childhood bond with his parents. He cannot become an adult as long as he remains his parent's "little boy." When a 75-year-old mother says to her 50-year-old son, "You'll always be my little boy," he's in trouble.

Obedience/Following the Rules:
The Good Boy is accustomed to following the rules and doing what he is told. Following rules without question and being obedient are ways that we learned to navigate through an often-times unpredictable and chaotic world. Being obedient helps us divert attention from ourselves. If we do what we are told then no one is going to give us a hard time—they might even leave us alone.

However, the consequences of such behavior can be detrimental to our emotional growth. In his *Twelve Rules of the Road*, Sam Keen cautions, "Don't obey. Obedience is a virtue for children, not adults." Adults have the capacity to question their world, including questioning the rules, and to not obey those rules if they believe that by doing so, they will compromise some part of their integrity and wholeness.

Summary:

The healthy gay man rejects the notion that he must remain subordinate and lets himself be something other than just nice. He gives himself permission to be a multidimensional being which, depending on the situation, can include being confrontational, tough and oppositional. He actively learns how to express his anger in healthy and appropriate ways—including righteous indignation when necessary. This does not give him license to plow through his world in a rageful tempest, nor should it condone bitchy, passive-aggressive behavior. Rather, he must learn how it feels to be in his anger, first by acknowledging that he has reason to be angry, and then to find healthy, productive ways of expressing it.

THE NARCISSIST

On the surface the narcissist is brash, exhibitionistic, self-assured, single-minded, often exuding an aura of success in career and relationships...In fact, the narcissist's personality is based on a defensive false self that he must keep inflated, like a balloon, in order not to feel the underlying rage and depression associated with an inadequate, fragmented sense of self.

— *The Search for the Real Self*, James Masterson, p. 90.

The Narcissist is the part of the *Puer* that has great difficulty connecting to his world. True connection involves the ability to get beyond one's own immediate needs and personal situation in order to be aware of and attend to life outside of oneself. The Narcissist remains in an "I" centered reality. His needs are all that really matter. Such egocentricity makes it extremely difficult for this kind of *Puer* to connect to or bond with other people.

In recent years, the term narcissism has become one of those pop-psychology buzzwords that has made its way out of the therapist's office and into mainstream American culture. It has taken on a seemingly all-encompassing and generic meaning. As with any such trend in language development, the meaning becomes diluted and the word soon loses its true essence.

The term originally came from Greek mythology. Narcissus was the son of the river god Cephissus and the nymph Leiriope. He was a very beautiful boy. His mother, Leiriope was told by the seer, Teiresias, that if Narcissus did not look at his own features, he would live a long life. Narcissus heartlessly rejected many suitors, including the nymph Echo and his lover, Ameinias. He sent Ameinias a sword which he then used to kill himself. This callous act incurred the wrath of the gods and Artemis caused Narcissus to see himself in the reflection of a pond. He fell in love with his reflection and thus was prevented from ever loving another. Eventually, overcome with grief, he took his own life and from his blood sprouted the flower that bears his name ("Narcissus," Encyclopedia Britannica Online).

Although the term narcissism has come to mean something along the lines of *loving oneself too much*, in its truest sense, it means just the opposite: Narcissism is the *inability to genuinely care for anyone,* including and most importantly, *the inability to care for and love oneself.*

The Diagnostic and Statistical Manual of Mental Disorders (DSM-IV) defines narcissism as "a pervasive pattern of grandiosity, need for admiration, and lack of empathy that begins by early adulthood and is present in a variety of contexts" (p. 658). Narcissism includes difficulty in connecting and committing, and in its most extreme form, can lead to a solitary and lonely existence.

A person with strong narcissistic features will often seem to be "in-love" with himself, sometimes giving the air of being totally self-absorbed, or in extreme cases, egomaniacal. Such qualities merely represent an outward manifestation of a well-developed façade fueled by grandiosity—a defense mechanism related to early psychic wounding—that covers up low self-esteem and feelings of worthlessness. It is important to remember that Narcissus fell in love with his *image*, not with himself.

Narcissism, like many other psychological conditions, is not necessarily an "either/or" proposition—*either one is a Narcissist or one isn't.* Instead, narcissism needs to be viewed on a continuum with most people falling somewhere on that continuum. In other words, everyone displays, at various times, narcissistic behaviors and attitudes. Interestingly, gay men often tend to show stronger narcissistic tendencies than heterosexuals. This doesn't mean that we are intrinsically less healthy; however, it does speak to our depth of wounding. So, why are some gay men higher on the narcissistic scale?

Here's a brief and somewhat oversimplified explanation of what creates unhealthy narcissism and how it relates to the gay experience. Narcissism begins at an early age, within the first three years of a child's life when his identity is being formed. In those years, it's normal for the child to exhibit an attitude of self-absorption and specialness. (Children, by their very nature are "I" focused—it's all about *me, me, me.*)

However, the way in which the child's world responds to his "healthy narcissism" is what determines whether he will advance beyond that developmental stage and form a realistic self-identity. For healthy development to occur, his specialness and grandiosity will be tempered through time with the normal disappointments and blows of life, thus allowing the child to understand, as he matures, that he is not so special after all. Abnormal development will occur when his primary parental figure tries either to squelch his natural grandiosity or to inflate it. Either of these responses are what can lead to a narcissistic disorder later on in life.

To further explain, a parent crushes a child's natural grandiosity by constantly criticizing the child's attempt to act out his healthy narcissism: *Stop bragging, Who do you think you are? You think you're pretty smart, don't you? You little show off.* His sense of self is destroyed and he has to create a *seemingly* strong façade to hide his empty core. This façade, however, is a fragile, paper-thin shell that is easily shattered. Thus when confronted with disapproval, he is unable to protect himself from his feelings of unworthiness. The fragile structure that the narcissist creates partly explains why it is so hard to confront him on his issues; he often crumbles and the other person may feel tremendous guilt for having caused such pain.

It is equally damaging when the parent inflates the child's grandiose view of himself with overly supportive and unrealistic messages such as: *You're the most gifted kid in this world, You're the smartest boy in school, You can't play with them, they're not as good as you are.* When these messages are used excessively, they prevent the child from learning a more realistic view of himself that the world would otherwise provide.

A third way that narcissism may develop is with the truly gifted child. This child's grandiosity is not tempered as much by his environment as the more normal child, and thus the outcome is more closely related to the over-supported child. His environment will actually *support* his feelings of specialness, rather than modify them. He continually receives feedback from his world that he is truly special. Eventually, he will come to believe this feedback whether it is the entire truth about him or not. Thus he will grow up relying on the outside world to reflect back to him his sense of self worth.

An example we may use is the successful and talented performer. He may have a very dysfunctional life, but when he is in front of an audience, the audience reflects back to him his sense of self and he feels loved and accepted totally. His fragile sense of self is inflated and he feels alive, but when he leaves the stage or the limelight of his fans or is panned by a critic, he deflates.

We think it is especially important to examine this possibility within a gay man's development. In a relatively healthy family, when a child is especially talented and creative, it is natural for his family to support and encourage his abilities. But when the child is gay, sometimes his talent is not necessarily in the area that the family wants to support, such as: a dancer, designer, singer or artist.

What happens to the fragile, developing identity of the child in this situation? It is obvious that often the child's sense of self is weakened and he will need to work harder in establishing a façade that is acceptable to his world. His true identity will be buried deeper and deeper in his psyche. (This is another reason for the importance of "coming out," so that one's inner sense of identity corresponds to one's outside world.)

In addition, not only is the gay child's creativity not supported, but also it is actively damaged by the condemnation that he faces from his immediate environment and the world at large. Here the gay child is doubly injured at a very crucial time in his development. What can this child do to attempt to establish a more stable sense of identity? He will "…expend his energy, like Narcissus, in repeated seemingly selfish efforts to obtain what he lacks" (p. 90, Satinover).

Furthermore, what often occurs is that little attention is given to his sense of differentness (i.e. his gayness), so this aspect gets squelched. He begins to feel invisible in this differentness since no one is acknowledging that he really is "different." Such differentness may include how the gay child thinks, perhaps drawing more heavily on his emotional and intuitive capacities than a straight boy would, how and with whom he chooses to play (e.g. with dolls and imaginary friends rather than with guns and other little boys), and how he behaves—perhaps with more feminine mannerisms. Most likely, his world, (i.e. Mom and Dad) are seeing these behavioral and attitudinal differences, but they are not talking about them. Or if they are, they're doing so in a clandestine manner, apart from their gay child. This can create severe disturbances in the gay child's ability to form a healthy relationship with himself.

Since our gayness was not discussed, we were not validated. Our sexuality remained this essential and *invisible* component of our being. So what most of us did to defend against the pain of invalidation was to react to this invalidation by making our specialness something very secretive, something that only we would know about, something that only we would understand about ourselves. This process of going "underground" with our identity fueled our sense of being special (in a covert and very personal way) rather than allowing us to come to a place of normalcy with our differentness, our sexuality.

Given all this, is it any wonder that most of us gay men have never really learned to love ourselves and that we might tend to display above normal levels of narcissism? Since we never got the chance to believe that who we were was OK and worth loving, we did not form a core belief of "okayness." In the early years, our sexuality was most likely treated as a non-issue: *my differentness was not seen, and therefore it did not exist.* Once we began school, our differentness often made us the target of homophobic persecution. The end result of years of such oppression is anything but self-love; all too often what we are left with is an ample amount of self-hatred and low self-esteem.

Then add to this mix the fact that most gay men don't get the experience of being a parent. For many people (most of whom are straight), raising children *can* be a primary method of healing innate narcissistic tendencies. Parenting can be a fundamental component in learning how to genuinely care for another human being, to get "out of" oneself and to see beyond one's own needs.

Clearly, while parenting does not automatically heal narcissism, it can provide *an opportunity* to do so. Sadly, all too often, when parents have not done their own work, they will use their children as extensions of their own egos. In such cases, having children actually serves to fuel the parent's narcissism, rather than to diminish or heal it. The parent must be conscious enough to take advantage of such an opportunity or it will be lost. Since many of us gay men are not going to have children, statistically speaking, we must find alternative pathways to heal our narcissism.

Of those, we believe the most effective and expedient is through psychotherapy. Psychotherapy, when effective, can offer the gay man an opportunity to form a meaningful connection (in this case with the therapist) and to use that connection to serve as a model for what he can begin to find more of outside the therapy office. Disconnection is a hallmark of narcissism; learning how to connect is what allows us to heal our narcissism.

CHARACTERISTICS OF THE NARCISSIST

The Narcissist embodies some of the most tragic characteristics of the *Puer*:

- Inability to care for self or others
- Lack of connection to one's world
- Inability to sustain a relationship
- Ending up alone

Inability to care for self or others:

The narcissist has never learned to truly care for himself. As with Narcissus, who was fixated on his reflection (image), the narcissist invests huge amounts of energy in caring for the image rather than his true self. Herein lies the dilemma: If a person is genuinely unable to care for himself, he will not be able to care for someone else.

Care of one's self would include an acknowledgment of one's shadow, an acceptance of one's limitations and shortcomings, permission to make mistakes and not be perfect, and empathy for one's own suffering. For the narcissist such genuine self-care is all but impossible.

The narcissist is so preoccupied with maintaining his façade of self-importance that he is unable to know how to genuinely care for, or respond to, the needs of those around him. He is much more versed in taking from his world rather than in giving back. He expects others to take care of him, and because of a strong sense of entitlement, he believes this is what he deserves. This aspect of the *Puer* likes others to pay his way, pick up after him, clean his house and cook his meals. Whatever the manifestation of his entitlement, he has difficulty extending himself to others, in doing his share of day-to-day tasks, in offering his time as a volunteer, or in nurturing those around him.

Lack of Connection to One's World:

The narcissist often has great difficulty forming meaningful connections in his world. Kyle was one such person. He complained that "the phone never rang" and he had few friends, although he felt that he was a likeable person. He had lost several important people to AIDS, including a lover of four years who had died the previous year. When Kyle talked about this lover, he stated that he really missed him. On the surface, this could look like a grief-related response, but when asked to explore "missing" further, he explained that he didn't feel very sad about the loss nor did he think about him very often.

The truth was that Kyle had little connection with anyone and while he could admit to missing his lover, it was more about his being alone, rather than a true sense of loss for someone he loved. If we are not connected to ourselves, we cannot connect to or love another.

Inability to Sustain a Relationship:

One of the main characteristics of narcissism is an inability to sustain meaningful relationships. Many gay men who struggle with such a situation may not have healed their early narcissistic wounding. As they get older, if their narcissism remains untreated, they will be more inclined to resign themselves to a solitary lifestyle, having successfully convinced themselves that being alone is really the way they prefer to live.

Take Jake, for instance. A former client, we ran into Jake not too long ago at a party. He talked about having finally come to terms with being alone, that he was happy with himself and that's all he needed. "I'm over trying to be in a relationship—it's just not for me. It's just too much work, and I'm not willing to keep looking." If he found someone to be in relationship with at some point, that would be great, he told us, but in the meantime, he was "totally content" being single.

On one hand, Jake's feeling at peace with being alone could be viewed as quite healthy. However, on the other hand, he may have been using this position as a defense against his loneliness and his inability to find his way out of that labyrinth. Jake could have been mistaking this newly found self-acceptance for some kind of psychological destination, rather than being able to see it as just another stop (albeit a very important one) along the path of psychological development. If so, he had set up a belief system whereby he rationalized his aloneness instead of seeing it as an issue that might need more attention. In fact, given what we knew about Jake, his aloneness was probably more about never having figured out how to be in relationship than about genuine self-love. Jake's primary problem, we believed, remained his disconnection.

Ending Up Alone:

Narcissism, if left unhealed, can often result in the gay man choosing, consciously or otherwise, to remain alone. There are many gay men who fall into this category. They are often bright, attractive, talented men who, at age 40, 50 or even 60, are still single. Some have never been in a relationship. Others may have had a series of short-lived ones usually not lasting more than a few months. They have searched, sometimes for years, to find a relationship, and without success, they have ended up alone. Others may have given up the search years ago.

Often they have decided that they would rather be single. Such a conclusion is not only a sad commentary on the gay experience; it is as well unnecessary. If these gay men were able to heal their narcissism, they could greatly improve the quality of their lives and increase the chances of finding a sustainable relationship. That is, if they could learn how to make meaningful connections, to care for someone else in a deep and lasting way, and to begin to empathize with themselves (including coming to an understanding of the pain that they have experienced) they might not have to live out lives of isolation and quiet desperation.

Instead, they could begin to form relationships and build community that would add richness and meaning to their lives, and to give them a sense of belonging and a purpose within their world.

While long-term relationship should not have to be the ultimate goal for all gay men, it does appear that most of us are in search of it. Whether or not this is one's desire, an intrinsic longing within the human heart seems to be for connection and to be known in a profound way by at least one other person in this world. Like Narcissus, as long as we remain fixated on our reflection and not able to see our true self, deep connection cannot occur.

THE ADDICT

The Addict is that aspect of the *Puer* that controls the gay man's life through addiction. An addiction is a relationship to a substance or process (behavioral and/or psychological) used in excess, and is the single most life-threatening *Puer* characteristic for all of us. John Bradshaw defines addiction as any pathological relationship with a mood-altering experience that has life-damaging consequences. Practically anything can be used addictively—anything that we use or do to avoid feeling. Thus any substance or process can become addictive. It all has to do with one's relationship to that substance or process: frequency of use, reasons for use, and consequences of use. All addictions, we believe, are the result of the *Puer* still being in control.

We all have addictions and it is vital to our process of Initiation that we acknowledge what they are. In this way we can learn to take control of the addictive behavior rather than the addiction remaining in control of us. Becoming aware of an addiction and seeking assistance, whether in a therapist's office or a 12-step program, is another giant initiative step toward adulthood.

Addictions are generally divided into two main categories: *Substance* and *Process*. Let's take a closer look at these.

SUBSTANCE ADDICTIONS

Substance addictions have to do with what a person puts into his body. They include:

- Alcohol
- Drugs (prescription and recreational)
- Food (especially sugar)
- Nicotine
- Caffeine

Substance addiction is very prevalent in the gay world. It makes sense. We all have unhealed wounds, hurts and memories of injustice that we would rather not deal with, so it is easy to want to drink them down or smoke them away or even to use prescription drugs to numb the pain we feel inside. But the work that we have to do as gay men is to allow ourselves to experience whatever feelings we need to feel. As the saying goes in Alcoholics Anonymous, "We need to feel as bad as we feel." In other words we need to allow our feelings to have a voice.

What lessons do our feelings hold for us? What information do they have for us? Feelings are there to give us information about our world. Without access to all of our feelings, we can't navigate our world as efficiently. The saying goes, "There is no way out, but through." In other words, there is no way out of the feeling, except by going into it and fully experiencing it.

Addictions rob us of our wisdom. Robert Bly says that in order to be wise, we must have been betrayed. (He does not state it, but we believe that he is talking about betrayal in adulthood, not as children. Betrayal as children leads to lack of *trust* in the world, not wisdom). Addictions prevent us from transforming our betrayals into wisdom. They keep us stuck and victimized by our betrayals.

Another way of putting it is that we *need* all our individual history, including our pain and suffering, to be complete human beings. In his book *Fire In the Belly*, Sam Keen explains it this way:

To create a heartful mind I must continuously be unfolding the ongoing story of my life and thinking as an autobiographical self rather than as a neutral observer. In scientific thought it is legitimate to try to be objective, to turn one's self into an anonymous and value-free observer. But when we are wrestling with any decision involving fundamental beliefs and values, we only think well when we are in touch with *all the passions of our life.* [italics ours] When we must decide whether to marry, to have children, to get an abortion, to divorce, to manufacture chemical weapons, to retire, to put our aging parents in a retirement home, to undergo chemotherapy, we need to get distance from the immediate problem and consider what we should do *from the perspective of our entire life.* (italics ours) To know how Sam Keen should act (not how "one" or "anyone" should act) I have to review my past and revision my future, place the present moment in the context of my memories and my hopes. *I must think as a man who has a story.* (italics ours)

We need to be able to present to the world as men with a story. We have to use our *whole* story, not just the part we like or the part we want the world to see. We have to have access to *all of whom we are,* the shadow as well. When we are using substances addictively, we do not have access to our whole being. We cut ourselves off from our power source. If we want to live as Warriors, we cannot afford to live with anything less than our total being. We can no longer drown our stories in substances.

PROCESS ADDICTIONS

Process addictions have to do with *behaviors* that a person engages in to excess. They include:

- Love (Sex, Romance and Relationship)
- Codependence
- Work
- Gambling /Spending
- Doing a "Geographic"
- Perfectionism

We would also include on this list such activities as: exercising (skiing, pumping iron, dancing, running, swimming, cycling, golfing); obsessive thinking; fantasizing; cooking; volunteering; child-rearing; reading; meditating; housecleaning; T.V.; sleeping; going to bars; cruising; raging; worrying; gardening, confusion, and drama. And the list goes on...

It may seem confusing that such behaviors as listed above can potentially be addictive. What does it mean that skiing, dancing, gardening, child rearing can be addictions? Anything that is used repetitively to avoid consciousness is an addiction. Some things, in and of themselves, are addictive, such as heroin. While most of the activities stated above are not addictive, in and of themselves, it is *the way* that one uses such activities that they become addictive. We, as gay men, must become very honest with ourselves to figure out what we use addictively. Questions to consider that will help lead us in that direction are: Am I using this behavior to avoid dealing with the issues that are important in my life? Am I engaging in this activity to avoid certain feelings?

Sometimes, a person uses *many* of these activities and/or substances sparingly. Thus, he can conclude that he does not have any additions because he does not use *anything* to excess. But pay attention here! It may be that the combination represents a single addiction of many parts.

"Well, I drink a few beers some evenings, but not that often. Yeah, I smoke a few joints, but only on the weekends. Sometimes I work 16 hours and then work out at the gym or run to relieve the stress. My partner complains that I watch too much television, but I only watch sporting events. We have a pretty good sex life, but when he's not interested, I watch some porn and masturbate. However, I only go to the bar a few times a week and I rarely have more than a couple of drinks." This person can really fool himself that he has no addictions, but when strung together, it is pretty obvious that he may be living very addictively.

The Love Addictions:

In her very important work on Love Addiction, *Escape from Intimacy*, Anne Wilson Schaef, a leader in the recovery field, identifies three main types: Sex, Romance and Relationship.

The Sex Addict:

The high level of sex addiction found within gay culture is in great part the result of men's lack of initiation and letting their *Puer* dominate their sexual experience. The fact that we are defined by our sexuality should not necessarily imply that we are sex addicts. However, sexual promiscuity is a likely indicator of a gay man being a sex addict. The *Puer* rushes in and has sex immediately with someone who turns him on—often anonymously, often in public places; the mature gay man takes a close look at how he uses sex and with whom he has it.

Patrick Carnes, a leader in the field of sex addiction maintains that there are ten signs of sexual addiction:

1. A pattern of out-of-control behavior
2. Severe consequences due to sexual behavior
3. Inability to stop despite adverse consequences
4. Persistent pursuit of self-destructive or high-risk behavior
5. Ongoing desire or effort to limit sexual behavior
6. Sexual obsession and fantasy as a primary coping strategy
7. Increasing amounts of sexual experience because the current level of activity is no longer sufficient
8. Severe mood changes around sexual activity
9. Inordinate amounts of time spent in obtaining sex, being sexual, or recovering from sexual experience
10. Neglect of important social, occupational or recreational activities because of sexual behavior

It is not uncommon for gay men to report that they feel that sexual promiscuity reflects their very essence as gay men. Many feel that it is their right to be able to have sex with whomever, however, and as often as they choose. Commonly held arguments sound something like: *It feels good, so why should I worry about it? It's the way I most identify as a gay man.* Although these are both valid points, and such men may be very justified in their opinion, their promiscuity may be creating more liabilities for them than the freedom they are seeking.

The real issue here is not what we do in bed, but how we use sex. What needs to be addressed is not whether a lot of sex is good or not, but rather *how* promiscuity ultimately affects us. The problem with promiscuity is that it reinforces certain values that do not lend themselves to forming long-term relationships.

Gay men, across the board, have worked hard to find sexual liberation. Many of us spent years trying to suppress this powerful force and we got a lot of help from our world to do so. Then, in coming out, we were able to finally begin to accept and even celebrate ourselves as sexual beings. These have been hard-won battles for us all.

I have given up so much in my life and have worked so hard to accept myself as a gay man; don't tell me I can't have as much sex as I want! This commonly held view seems reasonable and quite understandable. After all, we do define ourselves by our sexuality, so if we don't perform sexually in a variety of ways and on a frequent basis, then who are we? Are we truly gay men? Expressing our sexuality is certainly healthier than suppressing it. But we must begin to find other ways to define ourselves, rather than solely on how we behave sexually.

When gay men meet and immediately become sexual, the delicate unfolding of a relationship has been thwarted and something precious has been lost. In other words, experiencing sexual intimacy immediately is more of a deterrent to a relationship than an asset. If a successful relationship develops in this manner, it will happen *in spite* of the couple having become immediately sexual rather than because of it.

At some point, that couple will have to back up and do the foundation work that should have happened in the beginning. Such foundation work includes learning how to communicate with each other, developing trust and a sense of safety—all the things inherent in any good friendship. Of course there are exceptions and certainly there are successful, long-term gay relationships that began immediately with sex. But the chances are, the sooner two people are sexual, the less chance they will have of developing a long-term relationship. James Masterson explains:

> In fact, a relationship that turns sexual early on, or even begins as a relationship, can abort the experimental process so crucial to building genuine intimacy. Sex has the power to blind the couple to the realities about each other and how they function together, so that the sifting and sorting out of positive and negative qualities in order to make an honest commitment based on knowledge and understanding never takes place.
> — *The Search for the Real Self*, p. 118.

The gay man who has one sexual encounter after the next, with hundreds if not thousands of partners (most of whom are strangers), and then wonders why he can't find a relationship that will last, needs to take a serious look at how his choices might be influencing that outcome. While healthy intimacy often includes sex, sex does not necessarily equate to healthy intimacy. Questions to consider on this issue are:

- Does my sexual promiscuity really serve me?
- Is it enhancing my spiritual and emotional well-being?
- Is it helping me to find and sustain a meaningful relationship?
- What does it mean to be as physically intimate as possible with another human being when that person is a total stranger?
- How does such behavior affect my ability to find a long-term relationship?

Difficult as they may be, these questions are important ones that we, as individuals and as a community, must begin to address. At no time are we speaking of morality here. We are not condemning gay men for having many sexual partners. We are not saying this is *wrong*.

Certainly, as gay men, we do not want to simply embrace the heterosexual model of relationship. We have a more expanded view of sexual behavior, and in many ways this behavior is very healthy. We have a freedom and openness about our sexuality that many straight people should be envious of. What we *are* suggesting is that our sexual behavior needs to be examined to ascertain whether or not it is serving us.

SLAA (Sex and Love Addicts Anonymous), and SCA (Sexual Compulsives Anonymous) are two 12-step programs that have sprung up in the last 15 years, and have helped countless numbers of people get a handle on their sex addiction.

■ ■ ■

Another aspect of sex addiction is seductiveness, which is often revealed through how one dresses. The *Puer* believes he should be able to dress however he chooses regardless of the situation. Certainly the world would be a boring place if everyone dressed like bankers and politicians, and although we do not want to discourage originality and creativity in dress, gay men must examine their motives for dressing seductively.

Adolescents dress to make a statement and they should. It is part of their individuation. *This society's not going to tell me what to wear!* When we continue to use dress primarily for the purpose of provoking, especially when it conveys more about our rebelliousness than our individuality, then the *Puer* is guiding us.

Provocative dress can actually say more about low self-esteem than about originality and individuality. When the gay man presents himself in a provocative or seductive manner, he is *asking* to be viewed as an object. The multi-faceted person he is becomes reduced to his physical characteristics. He is saying to the world, "Like me for my looks, not my total being."

Bobby consistently came to group therapy sessions complaining of his loneliness. He was a very attractive man and often wore clothes that exposed his underwear and accentuated his crotch. He complained that men constantly hit on him, stating, "All they ever want is sex." For months he was unwilling to explore the role he was playing in creating his own objectification.

Even though group members challenged him on his seductive dress, he continued to believe that he had no control over how men treated him. Finally a group member said, "Bobby, it's hard to get to know you because I can't get beyond your tight pants and your body piercings." This proved to be a pivotal moment for Bobby and he listened as other group members gave him similar feedback. In time, Bobby became more willing to entertain the idea that maybe there was a connection between his dress, being constantly objectified, and his loneliness.

The Romance Addict:

"…[N]o interpersonal or pseudo-relationship addiction has anything to do with love…The romance addict uses form as a 'fix'…Romance addicts are obsessed with the *accoutrements* of relationships, *not* relationships" (Schaef, p. 47, 50). Often this kind of *Puer* will be more invested in the fantasy of a relationship and less in the actual reality. He will always want the setting to be perfect, the mood to be right and the wine of the finest quality. It does not matter much about the depth of the situation. The romance addict is only interested in the *form* of the relationship.

This is an interesting situation for many gay men who are often known for their taste and aesthetics. It may be easy for them to get lost in the form and not notice the substance. One of the ways gay men have survived is in paying attention to detail. Making sure that everything is as perfect as they can make it. That way it will be harder for the world to find fault with them. This can mislead them into thinking that this is the most important part of a relationship—how it looks!

The Relationship Addict:

The *Puer* is often a relationship addict. He needs a relationship to reflect back to him the identity he lacks. The *Puer* often projects missing pieces of himself onto his partners, and even though on the surface it may appear that he is relating to the other, he is actually relating to his own reflection, (see "The Narcissist").

Relationship Addicts move through relationships quickly; every few months they may have a new boyfriend. For adolescents, this behavior is normal and important; they are learning about relationships, experiencing the excitement of winning and the pain of loss.

Many gay men, motivated by their *Puer*, continue this pattern well into their 30's and beyond. They have no idea how to form lasting relationships, so they move from one person to the next. They thrive on admiration from others, and as long as the partner is willing to make them feel "special," a relationship is possible. When the partner begins tiring of the one-sidedness of the relationship, this type of *Puer* loses interest.

Relationship Addicts are terrified of being alone. They will have a new person in the wings before they leave an old relationship. Quite often that means they don't really grieve the loss of the last relationship before they move into the excitement of a new one. Of course, this means that they will carry all their old issues into the new relationship. No matter, at least they're not alone! These men are also very controlling. Since they depend on the relationship to define themselves, controlling all aspects of the relationship is of utmost importance.

The Relationship Addict tends to look for love in all the wrong places, with all the wrong people. He does this because he's never developed a healthy sense of what love is. If he grew up in an environment that did not support and accept him in his differentness (i.e. his gayness), chances are he will later mistake this lack of support and acceptance for love.

Think of love as a kind of energetic frequency. This frequency is based on what we received early on from the people who were supposed to teach us about love—namely our parents. Through these teachings, each of us developed our own particular "love frequency" that we would later unconsciously look for in others. Sometimes these teachings were correct and helped us to develop a healthy sense of what love is, or what we call a "positive love frequency"; other times the teachings were incorrect and led us to form a faulty sense of what love is, or a "negative love frequency."

As children, we became very familiar with the love frequency that we received from each of our parents. If, for instance, our father was unaccepting and emotionally distant, we developed a familiarity with that particular frequency. As adults, we may unconsciously seek out a similar frequency, one that we recognize from childhood. In this case, we would respond favorably to unaccepting and emotionally shout down men, being familiar with this frequency and then mistaking it for love.

Keep in mind that all this happens on an unconscious level. Understanding this perspective can help us to see how we might seek out men who are least likely to be able to love us. In short, if our fathers (or mothers) were not able to genuinely love us, we might be looking for love in the wrong places.

Codependence:

Codependence is the process of becoming so entangled in someone else's life that one begins to lose sight of one's own needs, boundaries, feelings and thoughts—in short, one's identity. Gay men make some of the best codependents in the world because they learned at an early age to put their needs aside, not to have boundaries, to forsake their own feelings and not trust what they were thinking in order to be accepted and valued (i.e. *not rejected*) by others.

Although codependence is a "process" addiction, it is as life threatening as any substance addiction. John Lee defines codependence as the unequal, unfair exchange of energy. He says it is as if someone has a straw in another's solar plexus and is draining that person dry.

Since many self-help books on codependence have been written in the last 15 years, we will limit our exploration of this topic. One of the best books that we know of regarding codependence and its treatment, and one that we often refer to clients, is *Codependent No More* by Melody Beattie.

When we are operating in our Adult ego state, we know how to develop and sustain intimate relationships. We know how to hold our friends in our consciousness even when they are not present. We understand that relationships unfold and grow with time and require deep care and attention.

Work Addiction:

Of all the process addictions, the one that remains the most overlooked, minimized, and underreported in our society is work addiction. Since we live in a workaholic society, it only stands to reason that we would be encouraged, supported, and highly rewarded for partaking in such an addiction. It is not uncommon within the corporate world, the sector of American business where so many people are now working, to be expected to work 60, 70 or 80 hours per week, five to seven days a week, 50 weeks out of the year.

Ironically, many of our colleagues see nothing wrong with this kind of schedule, and when challenged on its health, may become defensive and quick to support its merit. "It's what I have to do so I can retire in 10 years." In the meantime, as they're overworking their way toward retirement, or greater prestige and fame in their field, they may be missing a big part of life.

Gambling/Spending:

It's easy to see how gambling and spending addictions are reaching epidemic proportions within our society. In New Mexico, evidence of this can be seen by the increasing number of casinos on many of the Indian pueblos. Here it's called "Gaming" (the power of euphemism to promote denial!). And New Mexico is not unique.

Some people who are not addictive personalities gamble for fun, a few times a year, but there are those who spend an inordinate amount of time and money in front of a slot machine or at a black jack table. They are completely distracted from the reality of their lives. Winning is always seen as the goal, but the truth is that the entire experience is a distraction in the same way that any addiction is.

As well, spending in all its myriad forms whether it's shopping on line or in the mall is an activity that many Americans, not just gay men, are highly addicted to. Before the Internet, we were fast becoming a "Mall culture." Now, with e-shopping, we are becoming a culture of at-home shoppers. Whatever the venue, if we shop in order to mood-alter or to find some kind of meaning in life, we are probably engaging in some form of spending addiction.

Doing a Geographic:

In the 12-step program there is a concept called "doing a geographic." Basically what this refers to is the belief that the grass will be greener on the other side of the fence. That all we need to do is move to that greener pasture and our life is finally going to be okay. There's no consideration in this thinking that we're going to take all the problems with us to that new pasture that we have yet to resolve in the old one.

Of course, there is always the initial excitement of a new environment. The first six months or so can be very distracting as we learn our way around and discover the uniqueness of that place. But after the blush has worn off, what we find is that things are pretty much the same and that the move has solved very little. Maybe we found a better job or maybe the new environment is more beautiful than the old, but the core issues that we were trying to escape are still there staring us in the face.

The Addict shows a constant need for change—including work, living situation and relationship. Bill, a registered nurse, goes from one job to another. After several months, a job becomes boring and he moves to another. Since nurses are in high demand, he's able to do this. Bill is also a jeweler, artist, and computer analyst; he cannot commit to any specific direction. Once a project becomes mundane, he quickly loses interest and moves on. There is always the concern that something will be missed if he commits to one path. In fact, this is true. Every time we make a choice, we eliminate another. The adult realizes this is the way life works; we will not be able to experience everything in this lifetime. So we grieve the things we cannot experience and celebrate those we can.

Perfectionism:

"At the center of an addiction is, in one form or another, a radical betrayal of trust."
— *The Ravaged Bridegroom*, Marion Woodman, p. 38.

Dan Jones, *What Makes a Man a Man,* uses the term "flawlessness" in his explanation of perfectionism. He says that "One of the difficulties with trying to be flawless is that you can never admit a mistake, so you can never apologize and be forgiven…[and] the essential quality of savvy is gained from the experiences of trial and error, and if we have to be flawless, we'll be too frozen to take risks and learn savvy" (p.75).

Marion Woodman explains that the addiction to perfection is the most dangerous addiction one can have. The addiction to perfection is a killer.

The problem is that one can never measure up to such a distorted standard. We will always be a failure in everything, since we can *never* do *anything* perfectly. We will carry our shame around because on some deeper psychological level, we know our perfectionism is a lie, we know we are not perfect. But if we can fool at least a few people, then it is worth it, but at what price?

The Perfectionist finds it unacceptable to be anything less than flawless. The man stuck in the *Puer* continues to recycle old, self-defeating messages that tell him that, if he makes a mistake, he's bad, stupid, or worthless. The *Puer* lacks the self-esteem to be able to say the words, "I've made a mistake." It takes great courage and is a function of the adult to admit a mistake. Therefore, mistakes are not a part of his image of himself.

Perfectionism is a road block to intimacy. How can a person be intimate with another and still maintain the façade of perfectionism? We find intimacy in the act of letting down our defenses, dropping our façade. If I am concerned with my image of being perfect, I will not allow anyone to see what's behind the veil. I will forever remain trapped in the false self that I have created to feel safe, but which now keeps me imprisoned and alone. What incredible bliss it can be to drop the façade of perfectionism and allow myself to make mistakes, be human, and thus be truly known by others.

For the gay man to become more fully adult, he must get out there in the world and let himself make mistakes. Rather than the mother admonishing her son as he leaves the house, "Be careful today", how different our world might be, if she were to say, "Take big risks and make a lot of mistakes!"

John Bradshaw says, "A task worth doing, is worth doing poorly!"

Summary:

Addictions come in many different forms. Sometimes they are well disguised; at other times they are obvious—at least to the people around us. Addictions are fueled by one's lack of Initiation, and remaining stuck in the *Puer* stage of development. The more we remain emotionally and psychically tied to our parents, the greater tendency we will have to continue to engage in addictive behavior. Recovery, if viewed as an initiative process, can often enhance one's ability to work on separating from one's family, of developing a stronger sense of self, and of finding one's personal power—all attributes of the Warrior.

Although it is understandable why addiction seems to be pervasive within gay culture, as long as we engage in addictive behavior, whether it's with a substance or a process, we will remain disempowered and unable to live as strong men. The way of the Warrior is about living as consciously as possible, and since addictions cloud our consciousness, we must be willing to look honestly at what our particular addictions are and be ready to commit to a plan of recovery.

THE IRRESPONSIBLE BOY

This part of the *Puer* shows a high level of irresponsibility to himself and to others. Examples of his irresponsibility are:

- Dishonesty
- Lack of Awareness
- Working below one's potential
- Lack of political involvement
- Rigidity

Dishonesty:

Dishonesty is one of the main characteristics of the Irresponsible *Puer*. One of the main ways he is dishonest is by hiding the truth about his sexuality. He believes that if people in his world really knew him, they would actually love him less. He lies about himself even when it would be just as easy to tell the truth. One of the big problems this *Puer* faces is that he believes that in order to be in his truth he *must be right*. If being gay is somehow wrong, then there's no way that he can reveal this information to his world. Better to stay in hiding than risk being authentic. This is a dangerous yet not uncommon belief.

One's truth is one's truth. It is not wrong, nor is it right. It is simply one's truth. It is all one has. When a gay man cannot live his truth, he has nothing. *This type of Puer thinks he can get around this by going deeper into the lies where the false self resides, but he comes up alone and empty time after time. When he surrounds himself with lies, the love the world offers does not nourish his soul, for he is being loved in his inauthenticity.* The Warrior values himself highly enough to know that he can and must "be in his truth."

Lack of Awareness:

The Irresponsible *Puer* often shows a lack of awareness because he moves through his world in a trance. Although he is capable of more awareness, maintaining the trance allows him to avoid painful feelings and his empty inner self. Examples of this *Puer* type would include not following through on promises, not owning up to mistakes, not paying bills on time or not at all, being late to appointments, or consistently misplacing keys, wallet and important papers.

This trance is a powerful defense mechanism that is also seen in abuse victims. Whether it is a result of abuse or lack of initiation, this defense is useful in protecting the inner self, when the individual has not worked through his emotions. Sometimes the *Puer's* lack of awareness is viewed as "laziness" or "not taking care of business", but it is, in fact, a very active and creative way of protecting oneself.

Working Below One's Potential:

The Irresponsible *Puer* has an aversion to work. This aspect of the *Puer* places work low on his list of priorities. Therefore, he will often settle for menial or unskilled jobs when, in fact, he could be capable of so much more. The illusion is that such jobs allow him greater freedom and less commitment. More "serious" jobs require a level of focus and attention that might affect his amount of playtime. Such work requires a long-term commitment inhibiting his ability to leave when he wishes, to move around more easily. Typically he fails to set stable and realistic work goals and often does not complete projects. He may begin a project with enthusiasm, but as the work becomes increasingly more mundane and laborious, his interest wanes.

Conversely, he also believes that he is special, he has a sense of grandiosity and entitlement. This basically means that he cannot take just any job because he deserves to have the best job. He resists starting at the bottom because he needs to be recognized as special in order to maintain his sense of self.

Pat, 42 years old, with a Masters degree in English, is still waiting tables at a restaurant. Whenever he is approached for a higher position, such as in management with the restaurant, he declines saying that he doesn't want the responsibility.

Billy, a 26-year-old, lives with Roger, 47, his self-proclaimed "Sugar Daddy." Roger, a successful ER doctor, often works 80 hours a week. Billy doesn't work and sees little need to change this set-up. Instead he goes to school part-time studying photography, which he's been doing since they met six years ago, and when he's not studying, he's at the beach cruising. He feels justified in continuing such a lifestyle since Roger agrees to it.

Lack of Political or Community Involvement:

The Irresponsible *Puer* can't be bothered with what's happening out there in the world because his own reality takes up all of his time. He is too busy surviving and maintaining an inauthentic life to bother with such involvement.

Social issues? What are those? Community involvement? I really don't like being in large groups.

On the surface, lack of community involvement might look like a form of individuation, but it is an example of an incomplete initiative process. A complete initiative process would include the third phase, *incorporation*, i.e., coming back into the community and being a contributing member.

For complete Initiation to occur, one must become an "adult member of the tribe." Today's equivalent of this is community and political involvement. The adult is capable of looking beyond his own needs and is able to consider the needs of the larger world. So-called "primitive" cultures helped their young accomplish this. The young boy entered the initiation process as a child and emerged as an adult member of his community. They understood that the child must die, so the adult may live.

While the recent *Inner child* movement has focused on protecting the child within so that he can eventually be integrated into the adult ego structure, Bly takes it a step further. He maintains that we need to *kill* the *inner child* because we can no longer afford to allow that child to be in control.

Rigidity:

Rigidity in behaviors and/or belief systems is a common characteristic of the child, and one exhibited by the *Puer*. Children often introject their parents' values, and as adolescents, completely reject them. Either way, rigidity can be the end result. This reminds us of the story of the mother who taught her son to always cut the end of the roast off before cooking it. The son asked her why and she replied that her mother had told her she should do it that way. When the son asked his grandmother about the reason for cutting the roast, Grandma explained that her cooking pot was not large enough to hold a whole roast. The mother had merely introjected her mother's instructions without questioning the reason. What happens with the uninitiated adult is that he has spent very little time investigating his own belief system and rules.

An adolescent's rigidity in behaviors and beliefs is most often the result of what he's learned within the family system. This rigidity expresses itself in political affiliations, religious beliefs, music appreciation, eating habits, dress and family traditions. The more rigid the belief system, the more insecure a person. Through initiation, the young man begins to create his own sense of security and thus to form his own belief system; some of it comes from the parents and society and much of it is created from within.

The *Puer's* rigidity is frequently demonstrated through behaviors such as narrow eating habits, or being a "picky" eater. There are a variety of reasons that people have certain eating quirks—some physiological, some historical, but mostly, we believe them to be psychologically-based and directly related to one's lack of initiation. Many people report that they've always disliked a certain food, such as peas, spinach, buttermilk, olives or onions, for no apparent reason. They might remember that when they were little, they got sick on fish or that their mom used to make carrots a certain way and they hated them. Or they'll talk about how their parents may have had certain food aversions or that they served only particular dishes. "My dad didn't like broccoli, so I don't like broccoli."

Certainly, there are realistic reasons, rather than just dysfunctional ones, for the absence of or preference for certain foods in families: economic considerations; cultural traditions; religious beliefs, to name a few. But more often than not, rigid eating habits are indicators of a rigid system of likes and dislikes being introjected from or in reaction to earlier events or people in one's life, without personal investigation.

Metaphorically, narrow eating habits might suggest an inability to leave home, retaining family loyalty, and/or not wanting to disappoint parents. A client recounted his mother telling him during a recent family visit, "You never used to like vegetables, so I would fix something special just for you." He understood that in order to maintain his special status and special connection to his mother, he had unconsciously continued to dislike vegetables well into adulthood. Such behavior is an obvious holdover from childhood and, if not made conscious, can prevent one from becoming an adult.

As an exercise, you might ask yourself: What food or foods do I really dislike? And two: Why do I really not like that food? If you are completely honest, there's a strong possibility that the dislike originated in your childhood.

The initiated adult does not say, "Ugh, I hate broccoli," nor pick the mushrooms out of the spaghetti sauce. The *Puer* does this in an effort to establish his independence and uniqueness. The adult might have food *preferences,* but he eats what is on his plate. (A note about vegetarianism: many people are vegetarians because of legitimate and healthy reasons, religious or moral beliefs, or food allergies. However, vegetarianism can be the result of being stuck in the *Puer* and have little to do with an adult-formed belief system or biochemistry.) Remember, the purpose of this investigation is to become more conscious of *Puer* tendencies, so one must examine the motivation behind eating habits—whatever they might be.

THE OPPRESSOR

The Oppressor is that part of the *Puer* who, having forgotten about his early wounding and specifically how he was hurt by others, has become one of those people who now oppresses others. Gay men, who have not found a recovery process through which to heal their early wounding, will often become as severe an oppressor as those who once oppressed them. There are certain environments where gay men congregate where such oppression seems to be most pronounced—places like the bar, the gym or the beach.

In the last few decades, places like South Beach, Puerto Vallarta, Fire Island and Provincetown have become hot spots for gay men from the United States, Canada, and Mexico. During vacations, we've had a chance to observe and interact with gay men in these beach milieus.

Generally, gay men love to size each other up according to physical characteristics. Oftentimes, those with gym bodies get much quicker acceptance than those who have just normal looking bodies. Those who don't measure up at all are often ignored and made to feel invisible.

There is a brutality in this objectification that leaves many of us with a feeling of being "less than." After much discussion of this objectification phenomenon, we began to wonder: How did we go from being wounded little boys who people picked on and made fun of, to these grown men who now can do the same, and this time, to our own kind? It's a classic example of how the oppressed becomes the oppressor.

This same dynamic happens in bars. As a gay man enters a bar, all eyes turn his way, and then many quickly turn away. Chances are he, too, will try to make eye contact with those individuals he feels are appealing and just as quickly turns away from those he is not interested in. What's going on at a deeper level of communication? Many gay men can remember being on the playground and not being chosen to play the games the other children where engaged in, or maybe they remember the shameful feelings of being the last to be chosen to be on a team. How is the bar scene any different?

Bill enters the bar and immediately sees Sam sitting at the bar having a beer. He thinks Sam is really hot and maneuvers his way around to get Sam's attention. Sam looks up and then quickly looks away. He obviously does not think Bill is attractive enough. Bill has been rejected in a matter of seconds; he has been found undesirable in the blink of an eye. This is certainly a familiar experience in Bill's life. Actually he is used to this type of rejection. He will probably say, if asked, that it doesn't bother him, it's just part of the game.

This is objectification at its core. In a matter of seconds, a multi-faceted and complex human being has been examined and judged not to be adequate. Yes, it is true that he is only being judged as a sexual partner, but what happens for Bill on a deeper psychic level? How much damage to Bill's identity is done at that moment? Probably not a tremendous amount. Bill will not self- destruct because of this small rejection. But what toll does this rejection take when we add them all up week after week and year after year. Do the small victories cancel out these continual failures? Here gay men are doing the same thing to each other that has happened to them. When do we allow ourselves to stop the game of abuse completely?

It is common knowledge that most perpetrators of abuse have been the victims of abuse. While it does not necessarily follow that all abuse victims will become perpetrators, if these victims do not heal the wounds from the abuse, there is a greater probability that they may abuse others.

There are two main forms of oppression: oppression of someone else and oppression of self. Wayne Mueller goes even further and explains that we're kidding ourselves if we believe that we've stopped the cycle of abuse by not abusing others. In fact, we will not have stopped this cycle until we stop abusing *ourselves*.

Victims No Longer is a powerful exploration of "Men Recovering from Incest and Other Sexual Child Abuse." Mike Lew explains the symptoms of sexual abuse and the results that stem from this abuse. Since we deal with sexual abuse situations in our practice, when we initially read this book, we were reading it for professional reasons.

Lew wrote the book for men who have been incested or sexually abused. As we began reading, we realized that it could have been written exclusively for gay men because *most gay men have been sexually abused!* We couldn't believe that we had not realized this before. Let's examine this more closely.

As boys, we were abused when we were called names like sissy or queer; but we were *sexually* abused when the name-calling became: cocksucker, cornholer, or buttfucker. These epithets were referring to our essential nature. While it is certainly abusive to call someone an idiot or stupid or a dumbshit, when gay men are called cocksuckers, they are being attacked at a very basic level—their *sexual identity*.

Lew identifies "frequent issues and problems faced by incest survivors" and we include a partial list here from his book that we believe pertain to many gay men, regardless of whether they have been *overtly* (in the traditional sense) sexually abused or not:

- Anxiety, panic attacks, fears
- Depression
- Low self-esteem
- Shame and Guilt
- Inability to trust
- Fear of feelings
- Violence
- Discomfort with being touched
- Compulsive sexual activity
- Sexual dysfunction
- Hypervigilance
- Social alienation
- Inability to sustain intimacy

We gay men seem to have this uncanny ability to forget about the years of oppression that we experienced as boys in an often times homophobic world, and then carry on with our lives as adults as if none of that early wounding ever occurred. What happened to all those years where we were shamed and taunted, the last to be picked for a team, or publicly humiliated by a peer? Usually what happens is that we bury the pain and hurt of the years of trauma and abuse, or we split off from it and move into a kind of pretend mode where we try to convince ourselves that it wasn't really all that bad. *After all, everyone had a hard time growing up.*

What we observe in gay milieus, whether it's the bar scene, at the beach or in the gym, is that there is a certain pecking order that is based on physical characteristics, and that all gay men that enter into this milieu are sized up and either accepted or rejected based on their physical appearance alone. Those that are sufficiently buffed are granted entry; those with ordinary to out-of-shape bodies can be treated like non-entities. There is elitism within this group dynamic that accepts some and shuns others. We, of all people, should know better than to shun our own kind, but nevertheless it happens.

The Oppressor often uses his unresolved anger to control and shame those around him. He may often be a bitch. Examples of this can be seen in the use of campy, acerbic, stinging humor. "Old Queens" have developed a reputation for such behavior; it's often not only supported but also encouraged within gay culture. The degree to which a gay man becomes a bitch is directly proportional to the depth of his unacknowledged rage. Oppressors are bullies. They may attempt to gain the upper hand through intimidation or coercion. Although they may pride themselves on being strong men, they are anything but. Underneath a thick bravado is a scared little boy who is deathly afraid of being re-injured.

PART IV

TRANSFORMING BETRAYAL INTO WISDOM:

The Journey of Initiation

In reaching out to grasp a troublesome past,
we cease to be at its mercy,
and the more we reach to make ourselves a witness to the past,
the less we are its victim.
— *Healing from the War*, Arthur Egendorf, p. 73.

The next step in a gay man's journey of Initiation is to learn how to transform betrayal into wisdom. In order to do so, he must be willing to acknowledge how and by whom he has been betrayed, and then to begin to feel whatever emotions might not have been worked through regarding those betrayals.

According to Robert Bly, in order to be wise, a person must have been betrayed. If a gay man knows how to work with betrayal, he can metamorphose from a naïve boy to a knowing, powerful adult. The uninitiated man is drawn down by his betrayals into an abyss of powerlessness and victimization. An initiated man has learned how to use betrayal as a kind of "warrior fuel", how to transform life's seemingly crueler lessons into wisdom.

There is a story of a young anthropologist who goes into a remote village to find someone who can teach him about wisdom. He first goes to the hut of the oldest man in the village. The anthropologist knocks on the door of this man's hut and several moments later, a wrinkled and well-weathered man appears and greets the young anthropologist. "Can you teach me about wisdom?" asks the anthropologist. "You are the oldest man of the tribe, and therefore, I believe you must be the wisest." The old man looks at him for several moments and then speaks, "Young man, it is true, I am the oldest man of this village, but I am not the wisest. If you want to talk to the wisest man, then you need to go to the hut across the way. He is not as old as I, but he has suffered more, and through his suffering, he has become the wisest." What the young anthropologist learns is that wisdom is not so much determined by age, as it is life experience. Betrayal alone, however, does not make one wise. Like the wisest man of the tribe, we must learn how to transform it into wisdom.

Betrayal is what teaches us about life's dangers. It is the cosmic reminder to us that the world is not always a safe and loving place; that it also contains treachery, deceit and situations that are life threatening. Betrayals are the "shadow" lessons of life. They teach us about the darker side of humanity. They are potential gifts to higher consciousness, but in order to see them as such, we must learn how to withstand them. To live as Warriors, we must have learned how not to be destroyed by our betrayals, but instead, understand their value.

When a person is betrayed, he has basically one of two choices: to become bitter and mistrusting of the world and the people in it, or to use the betrayal as an opportunity to become wiser. The first choice moves him further into the role of victim; the second moves him closer to the Warrior. The Warrior understands that betrayal is an opportunity for spiritual growth and greater insight, which will lead him to a place of greater wisdom.

The victim sees betrayal as yet another example of life's unending unfairness. To choose the role of victim can be understandable and even necessary at times, but always it is at great expense to one's psychic development. The victim sees betrayal as some horrible thing that has happened to him over which he has no control; the Warrior sees betrayal as some horrible thing that has occurred in order to help him be stronger and more prepared to live in the real world.

Carlos Castaneda explains in *Tales of Power*, "The basic difference between an ordinary man and a Warrior is that a Warrior takes everything as a challenge while an ordinary man takes everything either as a blessing or a curse" (p.109). Finding one's Warrior goes far beyond just improving self: it holds the seeds of making great transformation within our world.

Making such a choice with betrayal is an adult function. That is to say, most children lack the ability to transform betrayal into wisdom. Their ego structures are usually not yet strong enough to be able to do so. In general, when betrayed, children lose trust in their world. They become cautious, isolative, and defeated.

Many of us demonstrated some or all of these qualities as a result of having been betrayed when we were children. It is understandable that we lost trust in our world. As adults, rarely are we true victims without playing some role in the process. Barring extraordinary circumstances—the Holocaust, war, severe accidents, police states—as adults, we must learn that we no longer have to play out the role of victim when something catastrophic happens to us. Instead, we can learn to use these experiences to become stronger and wiser.

BETRAYAL THROUGH HIV

All gay men live with HIV and AIDS, whether the virus now exists in their own bodies or in the bodies of those they love, live and work with, identify with, and sometimes fear. Being gay means being profoundly affected by the epidemic.
— In the Shadow of the Epidemic, Walt Odets, p. 14.

One of the most profound betrayals that hundreds of thousands of gay men have experienced in recent time is in becoming HIV+. It is certainly not the first betrayal for any; but arguably it is the most significant. After a lifetime of cumulative betrayals, first by family, then by school and community, and later in the work place and by society, the HIV positive gay man is now faced with the deepest betrayal of all—life itself. As with any betrayal, he has one of two choices: to become empowered by it and use it as a vehicle toward heightened awareness, or to become further disempowered and bitter.

To live as a victim with HIV might look something like this: isolation from the people who could most offer him care and support; an increase in unhealthy behaviors (unsafe sex, drug and alcohol abuse); staying uninformed about the latest medical treatments; or an unwillingness to identify and grieve the loss of the person he was before HIV.

To live as a Warrior with HIV is to view the disease as an opportunity for growth— spiritually, intellectually and emotionally—and to use this betrayal as an initiatory step toward manhood. This path ultimately can lead to wholeness, strength and power. The Warrior takes responsibility for his situation. This means that he does not beat himself up for having become infected, but rather that he comes to accept the reality of the situation—that he has a serious illness and inherent in any illness is a set of limitations. He recognizes that he is not responsible *for* the virus, but rather that he is responsible *to* the virus—a subtle, but absolutely vital, perceptual shift.

For the men in this category, they have learned to become more political and to defend their rights against the existing power structures. Many have become highly informed patients, actively involved in their health care. They have developed a better understanding of how they want their lives to look, and have learned to more fully experience the preciousness of each moment.

Ironically, by a twist of biological fate, HIV infection has become one of the most powerful initiative processes for some gay men. Clearly, no man made this decision with the conscious intention of finding his Warrior; but nevertheless, many HIV positive men have become stronger, more powerful adults, due to their illness.

As potentially transformational as we now know HIV/AIDS can be, both on the personal and collective levels, the disease has some definite limitations. Most obvious would be the men with HIV/AIDS, who have transformed this profound betrayal into wisdom, may not be around ten or twenty years from now to transmit their wealth of knowledge to the younger members of the community. Unfortunately, too many of these men with vision and talent (such as Paul Monette and Randy Shiltz), who could have been some of our most powerful elders, have already died. Clearly, we must find alternative and life-supportive processes for helping gay men become initiated, processes that are born out of a *conscious* desire to become strong men.

BETRAYAL THROUGH WAR

For once a man grants himself the freedom to be appropriately upset by what he has seen and done, his reactions subside quite naturally, and he experiences himself as "more himself." (p. 69)

Whether it is to acknowledge a wrong we committed, a long-overlooked personal shortcoming, a desire that has escaped our attention or seemed too loathsome to admit, with such insights we announce an expanded identity. In effect we say, "I now see myself as including what I used to leave out." (p. 121)
— *Healing from the War*, Arthur Egendorf

In recent times, one of the most striking examples of betrayal has been the Vietnam War. In *Healing From the War*, Egendorf asserts that the soldiers in Vietnam experienced the most profound betrayal possible. Their entire moral foundation was destroyed. Being young, many of them did not have a very strong moral foundation to begin with. They trusted that the government that sent them to war was certainly right and would not ask them to do anything that was in any way immoral.

Unfortunately, that was not the case and they were expected to do many immoral things and saw, first hand, man's inhumanity to man. Whatever moral foundation they possessed upon entering the war was completely destroyed by the outrageous inhumanity they witnessed.

It is interesting to note that the suicide rate of Vietnam vets since the *end* of the war is higher than the total number of causalities *during* the war. Such a statistic points to the fact that a vast number of men were unable to overcome the psychic devastation done to them because the amount of damage was too extensive. However, for those who were able to transform such enormous betrayal, a state of profound wisdom could be attained.

Each bit of retracing steps contributes by widening our grasp on what we've experienced, transforming memory from an intrusion to a reminder that the present is elastic and can expand to hold the time of our lives as a whole. In this way old pain is healed, but not because we forget. *The more amply we reach out to grasp our past, the more we can look on old pain gratefully, recognizing it as the instigator that provoked us into growing to encompass it* (Italics ours) (p. 74).

Only a small percentage of people who serve in combat ever attain such wisdom and it only happens after intensive self-examination. If you have ever met a war vet who has managed to turn his betrayal into wisdom, you will know it immediately and most likely not easily forget him.

We have often wondered where all those "wise" men in our parents' generation were hiding. Many veterans of World War II certainly had experiences that could have had a profound effect on their journeys toward wisdom. But it seems that they returned from the war uninitiated. Certainly they were more "worldly" than before the war, but where was the wisdom?

Susan Faludi explains, "The triumphant nation presumed that because he and his fellow GIs were the victors, they were the virtuous; somehow winning had cleansed them and their countrymen, absolved them of the need for contrition." (p.378). Our fathers "won" their war. They came home triumphant to celebrations and honors, but they had no opportunity to grieve the horrible losses of the war. They had killed Germans and Japanese. Were all of those men evil and vile? Were they all Hitlers and Himmlers? The answer is obvious. Many of them were just ordinary men, like our fathers—fighting for a cause.

Before the war, they had ordinary lives with families and friends and jobs and aspirations. Our fathers had killed many of them. But since our fathers were the *good* men on the *good* side, fighting the *good* war, there was no room for grief or contrition. Since these were absent, there was no transformation. Winning, which in turn, denied them an opportunity to grieve, prevented them from developing "wisdom" to pass on to their sons.

To further complicate the issue, the nation as a whole was not allowed to repent, to grieve. The only *right* conclusion that anyone could subscribe to was that it was a *good* thing that the Allies had won the war against *evil*. Our entire society lost the opportunity to transform its experience into wisdom. We remained an adolescent society.

However, there is a man from that war whose heroic journey does illustrate the ability to rise out of one of the most horrendous betrayals of all and become a deeply knowing individual. He was not a soldier though, but rather a holocaust survivor. Here is some of his story.

A PROFOUND EXAMPLE

Perhaps one of the best accounts of becoming a Warrior through betrayal is Victor Frankl's *Man's Search for Meaning*, an autobiographical account of surviving the holocaust. Frankl recounts his experience as a prisoner in Nazi concentration camps. Despite this unfathomable betrayal of the Jewish people by the Germans (as well as homosexuals, gypsies and other targeted groups), Frankl understood that his survival depended on his perceptions of his situation. He realized that no matter how much the Nazis stripped from him, dehumanized and tortured him, the one thing they could not take away was his intellectual/perceptual freedom, and in that way, he retained his independence in the face of the worst imprisonment imaginable.

In realizing the ability "to choose one's own way" (p.75), he gained his ultimate freedom and empowered himself as a Warrior. He was free to think and believe however he chose, and no Nazi could change that. Thus he could choose to have hope—hope that someday he would be free.

Frankl maintains that it was this hope that kept him alive and allowed him to survive one of the greatest atrocities in history. What Frankl accomplished was what any Warrior must accomplish—to see that there is choice within the depths of any suffering.

The more a person has experienced betrayal, the greater his chances are of becoming Warrior-like, but only if he has developed the ability to rise above these experiences, and comes to see them as "gifts" that help him move toward a greater understanding of himself and the world.

Transforming betrayal into wisdom is a process with three main components:

- Identifying the betrayal
- Feeling the feelings connected to that betrayal (most importantly grief)
- Working with someone who understands this process in order to make sense of the lesson(s)

The first component has to do with coming to terms with where, when and by whom one has been betrayed. Often when we work with clients, we will hear some of them say, "Oh, well, it wasn't that bad." Unless the minimizing of a past traumatic event is necessary for the client (due to a lack of readiness to confront deep pain), we might suggest, "Yes, it sounds like it really was pretty bad." Or, "Maybe it's time to let yourself begin to acknowledge that you were betrayed" (whether it was being rejected, abandoned, abused or otherwise).

The second is an emotive process and requires experiencing the breadth of feelings related to the betrayal and actively grieving the losses that resulted from that betrayal. There is no set time on how long this process takes. As a rule of thumb, the deeper the betrayal, the longer the time required for recovery.

The third component is receiving assistance in working through the process. This other person, who serves as a witness, must be someone who has an understanding of transforming betrayal into wisdom. Since he is already familiar with this territory, he can offer support and guidance.

We gay men, without exception, know first hand about betrayal—whether from being infected with HIV, losing a job on the basis of our sexual orientation, physically assaulted by deranged homophobes, or abandoned by our families. Precisely because of the amount and intensity of the betrayals we have experienced, if we can find an initiative path—one that will help us to transform these harsh lessons of life into greater wisdom—we will become some of the most powerful Warriors in this society. In time, some of us will become the leaders, the gay elders who will represent our community in the political, academic and spiritual realms. The gay community is in dire need of such Warriors—men who have survived and learned from their betrayals, men who can guide the younger ones and teach them how to transform their betrayals into wisdom.

COMING OUT

Feel the Fear and Do It Anyway

Coming out is *the* most important first step in any gay man's journey of Initiation. It is a symbolic separation from one's family through letting go of the false self (the persona he has identified with and that his world has known him to be) and embracing the true self—one's authentic gay essence. Walt Odets explains, *In the Shadow of the Epidemic,* that the gay child lives an inauthentic life. He develops a false self in order to survive in a world that is non-supportive and often actively hostile. Odets' thinking helps us to view the process of coming out in an entirely new light. In order to live authentically, the gay man *must* come out. He cannot live with this false self and survive any longer. His physical, psychological and spiritual life depends on it.

Coming out is a letting go of the old agreement that a gay man has had with his family since the beginning of his awareness of being different. This agreement has said, *My gayness will remain a secret.* Coming out is a move toward a new agreement that says, *I now want acknowledgment for my sexuality.* And even further, *I want to be seen in my wholeness—as a gay man, unashamed.* Until a gay man has come out to his parents and the rest of his family *as well as all the other important players in his world,* he cannot even begin the process of Initiation. Instead, he will remain indefinitely in a subordinate position within the family system, feeling "less than" and inferior.

Until all the important people in our world know this *essential* truth about us, we will be unable to live as Warriors. Coming out allows each of us to move from the realm of childhood—where much of who we were had to remain a secret—to the realm of adulthood where we no longer have to live in secrecy. It is a way of saying to the world, *Who I am as a gay man is good and worthy of celebration, and I want you to know about it. Hopefully we can celebrate this together. If not, I will celebrate with those who support me.* When he comes out, the gay man is breaking through his fear and shame, and proclaiming to the world his truth. Such behavior takes great courage, and many men are too quick to forget the amount of courage it required for them to express their truth.

There are several main principles in coming out that apply to all gay men:

- Feeling the fear and doing it anyway
- Differentiating between rational and irrational fears
- Not underestimating its importance
- Doing it for yourself first and foremost
- Letting go of the outcome
- Reclaiming your power
- Doing it as an act of love
- Seeing its spiritual purpose

The gay man must face his ultimate fear(s) about coming out and do it anyway. One of the best books we know of on helping people break through their fears, take risks, and live a more powerful life is: *Feel the Fear and Do It Anyway,* by Susan Jeffers. She asserts that, as human beings, we tend to wait until our fear has subsided before taking action; in fact, what we need to learn is to begin taking the action, even though the fear is still present. It is only through taking the risk (even if we're shaking in our boots) that we will be able to move beyond the fear that has kept us stuck.

When discussing the coming out issue with clients, we often hear: "I don't want to hurt my parents."; "She's just not ready to hear it."; "I'm afraid he'll leave me if I tell him."; or "They'd have to be pretty stupid not to know." These reasons (or rather excuses), however potentially accurate, are about putting the needs of the other person before their own. Underneath the seeming need to protect the other person from the truth is an attempt to avoid the fear—the fear of rejection and abandonment. What does it mean when a man is afraid to speak his truth in revealing his essence? *Who I am might kill my mother/father!*

Fear is an understandable and even necessary component of the human experience. Its purpose is to alert us to possible danger. Gay men have good reason to sometimes feel afraid; our world has often been unsafe. If living in the age of AIDS isn't reason enough for gay men to experience a certain amount of fear, then perhaps the fact that, periodically, one of us gets beaten up, tortured and even crucified is sufficient justification for a certain amount of anxiety. However, when fear becomes so great that it impedes a person's ability to function on a day-to-day basis, it then becomes problematic.

In order to better understand the nature of fear, it is important to make a distinction between two kinds: rational fears (which have a basis in reality); and irrational fears (things we are afraid of for no logical reason). A gay man must ask himself, *How rational is my fear that my family will abandon me, if I come out to them?* In some cases it may be; in most cases it is not. Only those fears that we are aware of—whether rational or not—can we begin to change. The ones that we resist acknowledging, that remain in our unconscious, are the ones that tend to create the most problems.

It is the *Puer* within each gay man that carries his irrational fears. The most common fear is, that if he comes out he will face dire consequences. If a gay man allows his *Puer* to be in control, he will have great difficulty coming out. He may find many "justifiable" reasons for not coming out, (not wanting to upset his family, not wanting to jeopardize his inheritance, believing it's not that important), but in fact, he may be terrified of being "found out."

It is vital that a gay man not underestimate or minimize the importance of coming out. The *Puer* believes that coming out is not important. Such a belief, however the *Puer* may try to justify it, can be catastrophic to the well being of the gay man. A gay man's survival depends on his ability to break out of the closet, to come out to his world. Some gay men will rationalize not coming out by saying things like, "My parents already know, so I don't need to tell them." But even if the parents do already know (and often times they do, albeit on a less than conscious level) that's not the point. The point is for the gay man to allow himself to actually say the words, *I am Gay,* as a way to actively live in his truth. Living one's truth is what characterizes the Warrior.

Juan, a man in his early 20's, explained his not coming out this way: "I've never actually told my parents I'm gay, but I've introduced them to my lovers, so I know they know." When asked if he might have fear about actually telling them, he said, "No, I just don't want to upset them." Chances are, Juan is not being honest with himself. If he had no fear, he wouldn't have a need to conceal such an integral part of himself from two of the most important people in his life. Furthermore, he is placing the issue of how his parents *might* react to this information above the importance of breaking through his own fear (and internalized homophobia) in order to increase his self worth. The first issue is totally out of his control; the second one is about self-empowerment.

A gay man must first come out for himself—and secondarily for the other person(s). As already mentioned, most people who have any sense of us (whether consciously or pre-consciously) already know that we're gay. Giving the other person the information isn't nearly as important as giving a voice to our deepest truth. We voice our truth about our sexuality to live in integrity, to heal our shame, to increase our self-esteem and to break the cycle of denial.

The gay man must let go of the outcome and embrace the fact that he has no control of how his world ultimately responds. His job is to tell the truth—the rest is out of his hands. If, however, the person he is sharing this precious information with cannot accept him, he needs to take a close look at what purpose it serves to keep this person in his life. There's an old saying that goes, "Better to be hated for who I am, than loved for who I am not."

Coming out is about reclaiming one's power. As long as a gay man fears telling the truth to his parents, by definition, they remain the ones in power. He is the powerless child, afraid to tell Mom and Dad that he was sent to the principal's office today. Furthermore, as long as he withholds the truth, he colludes with his world in allowing his sexuality to be a non-issue; that is, he stays an asexual being. While his straight siblings get to talk about their relationships and romantic trials and tribulations, he must remain silent—and sexless. *If a gay man's parents cannot accept his gayness, it is essential that he separate from them (physically and emotionally) in order to maintain his integrity and self-esteem.* He does his parents and himself a great disservice when he tolerates their homophobia, whether spoken or implied.

Coming out is an act of love. The gay man is showing tremendous care and compassion for himself when he reveals his secret. As well, he is offering the other person the greatest gift he can give. He is offering the gift of himself, of his true identity. Coming out is a life-long process that a man finishes only when there is literally no one left in his world who doesn't know that he is gay. Perhaps, in the best of all possible worlds, being gay would only be about our sexual orientation, but in the world we live in today, it is much, much more.

When we read or hear people say, "Being gay is only one part of who I am," we have to cringe. As a child, being gay affected every aspect of his life. It affected whom he befriended and didn't befriend. It affected what activities he engaged in and which ones he did not. In some cases, it even affected what he studied or didn't. Perhaps, some day, it will be only about sexual orientation, but until that day comes, it is internalized homophobia that makes a gay man say that his homosexuality is only one part of him.

And last, the gay man needs to consider that coming out is part of his spiritual journey. Deciding to live in the truth rather than continuing to live a lie is one of the most important sources of spiritual insight. "When you're confronting your own sexuality, you're confronting yourself at the very deepest level of your being—and it's in that deepest level of your being that your spirituality dwells as well" (Sweasey, p. 23).

Being gay is not about a life-style; it's about a way of life. It's about who a gay man is at his core. Being gay goes far beyond what a man does in bed with another man. Being gay is an entire life experience that sexuality is only one facet of. It's as much about spirituality or politics, innate intelligence or intuition, as what happens sexually.

Here's what Harvey Milk has to say about coming out:

> Gay people, we will not win our rights by staying quietly in our closets. We are coming out! We are coming out to fight the lies, the myths, the distortions! We are coming out to tell the truth about gays, for I am tired of the conspiracy of silence, so I am going to talk about it. And I want you to talk about it. You must come out. Come out to your parents, your relatives... (*The Mayor of Castro Street*, Randy Shilts, p.365.)

> Come out to your friends...if indeed they are your friends. Come out to your neighbors...to your fellow workers...to the people who work where you eat and shop...but for once and for all, break down the myths, destroy the lies and distortions.
> For your sake.
> For their sake.
> For the sake of the youngsters...(p. 368.)

BEYOND COMING OUT

After a gay man has told his parents (and family) the truth about his sexuality, the work has only just begun. Now he must be willing to look honestly at how their reactions to his coming out have influenced and continue to influence how he feels about himself.

Conrad's coming out experience illustrates this point. When Conrad came out to his parents they responded in very different ways. It wasn't until years later that he began to understand how their various responses had been influencing his sense of himself as a gay man.

Conrad's father was outwardly very angry and rejecting of his gayness. In fact, for the first 15 years of his relationship with Grant, his father would not allow Grant to set foot in their house. In Conrad's perception, his father became the designated homophobe since his behavior was so extreme, his hatred so palpable. To give more contextual understanding to his father's position, he had been a policeman in New York for 25 years, and his experience with homosexuals was restricted to arresting them in public bathrooms. To him, gay equated with criminally-deviant.

Conrad's mother, on the other hand, was much less overt about her homophobia. She was able to conceal it under the often-used maternal cloak, "Of course I love you—you're my son." But her behavior didn't always remain congruent with the lip-service she was paying his sexuality, his relationship, or his life. Because of her incongruity, it took Conrad years to see that her form of homophobia was as severe if not more so than his father's, because of its insidious quality.

Her unwillingness to read books and become better educated about the gay experience, her obvious favoritism toward her other (straight) children, and her refusal to ever discuss his gayness, all pointed to a deep and abiding judgment that her son was not okay. She let Conrad's father carry her shadow feelings about his homosexuality, while rewarding his straight brothers and their families financially and emotionally for being like her.

We have to look closely at the parent who merely tolerates our sexuality. They might not say they don't approve, but if we look at their behavior and attitudes, we may see that, in fact, they do not. Such an investigation might seem quite painful to consider, especially if we've gotten to the place with our parents that they have agreed not to make a big deal about "it." *Just as long as "it" doesn't get talked about, you get to remain a part of the family.*

For many gay men, this kind of quasi acceptance ("Let's just not talk about it, honey. It'll upset your father too much…") can be misinterpreted as a success in the process of coming out. *Okay, I've told them, they know, and now we don't have to talk about it ever again.* But we do have to keep talking about it, and if they don't want to listen, all the more reason for us to bring it up. This is not to say that we have to be in their faces or to confront them in a rageful manner. But we have to confront their homophobic responses, whether it's the "No Talk" rule (Yes, we know you're gay. Isn't that enough? Do we have to constantly talk about it?), an off - handed queer joke in our presence, not taking our gay relationships as seriously as our straight sibling's primary relationships, or any other of a multitude of homophobic and/or heterosexist responses that our families might give us.

In a way, Conrad's parents' responses (or lack of) represent the two most common approaches that most parents will take when they struggle with their child's gayness. His father was what he considered a raging homophobe. In many respects, although Conrad didn't know it at the time, he was the easier parent to deal with. His homophobia was out in the open. He did not like, understand, or approve of his gayness and he made no bones about it.

His mother's opinion of his gayness, on the other hand, had been much trickier to understand. On the surface, she would tell Conrad that she was fine with it, but her behavior indicated just the opposite. When Conrad first came out to her, she asked him to promise that he and Grant would never have kids. Although Conrad was shocked by her request, and did not respond to something so outrageous, he stuffed his anger and sense of shame, and allowed her to continue in her abuse.

Years later, on a number of occasions, Conrad confronted her, reminding her of this extremely homophobic statement (not to mention her rage), and she repeatedly told him that she had no memory of ever saying such a thing. But Conrad remembered, and for years, the hurt and shame found a place deep within him.

Did her request influence his decision not to have kids? He could not hold his mother completely responsible for their not having children, but he knew, deep down in his gut, that he had allowed her to influence him from becoming a parent. She saw him unfit to be a father on the basis of his sexuality alone; on some level, he had internalized that perception.

The more a parent disguises his/her homophobia, the more it confuses us and keeps us tied into a system that does not serve us. This is toxic to our souls. Here the Initiation work is to confront a parent rather than to tolerate and accept the homophobia. Parents need to be challenged. That's one of the ways they grow. We must be willing to teach them about ourselves and sometimes challenge them on homophobic beliefs and behaviors they may not even know they possess.

The psychic toll of allowing a parent not to accept our gayness can be great. "I know they love me, they just cannot accept my being gay." If people cannot love us for our gayness, they cannot truly love us. Is it acceptable for someone to reject us for the color of our eyes? What's the difference? *They love me, but they probably wish I were different.* Why do we let parents get away with that attitude? Why is it okay that they get to wish that we were not this way? This is the way we are, and there must be some very good and specific reasons; furthermore, why shouldn't our gayness be reason for celebration? *We are so proud that you are gay and you're our son.*

For many gay men, these words might seem ludicrous. But why? How many of us have parents who have so clearly and joyously affirmed our essence? At some core level, we believe this is really way too much to ask. But why do our straight siblings get this kind of carte-blanche acceptance and welcome? One has only to attend a straight wedding to see such acceptance played out in all its pageantry and ritual.

Coming out includes these three elements: honesty, courage, and faith. Finally the gay man gets the chance to be really honest with the people who matter most to him and who deserve his truth. Does he honor his parents with the truth or does he dishonor them by staying in the lie? To come out requires enormous strength because he is breaking major cultural, societal and familial rules in taking this action. Coming out requires taking a huge leap of faith into the unknown, risking even further rejection in what has sometimes been a lifetime of rejections. It is about trusting that he will live through the experience and come out on the other side, more whole and complete.

LEAVING HOME

More than Just a New Address

Children soak up both verbal and nonverbal messages like sponges—indiscriminately... Because they have little frame of reference outside the family, the things they learn at home about themselves and others become universal truths engraved deeply in their minds.
    from *Toxic Parents*, Susan Forward, p. 32.

Another important step in a gay man's Initiation is when he eventually leaves home. Leaving home is more than just the act of saying goodbye to Mom and Dad, getting in the car and driving away to a new home somewhere else. More importantly, leaving home requires a perceptual and attitudinal shift within the gay man, so that he comes to see his parents as two other people on the planet with their own strengths and limitations. He begins to understand that the people he once viewed as all powerful, all knowing beings, are mere mortals, however happy or miserable, with their own successes and failures, struggling to find their way along life's path.

Wayne Mueller, author of *Legacy of the Heart*, explains that we must grieve the death of our parents *as our parents*. In other words, in our mind's eye, they must die as our parents, so that we can see them as just two individuals in the world with their strengths and weaknesses, but no longer as super-humans or as gods.

As long as we think that we can never do it as well as Mom and Dad, we'll stay child-like, unable to find our *Inner Parent*. Not until we begin the work of letting go of the myth, the fantasy bond, especially if our parent(s) could not support us in the full dimensionality of our gayness, can we move toward realizing our fullest potential. This process of grieving the death of our parents is the essence of Initiation.

Whether one's parents are alive or dead makes no difference in leaving home. The parents we are referring to are those who live on within the psyche. They are the people who still have power over the son, influencing the decisions that he makes and affecting how he feels about himself. To become initiated, a gay man must let go of his family of origin, and find his place within the world of adults. Only after such a step has been taken will he be able to *re-enter* his family of origin as a decidedly new and changed person—as a powerful, self-actualized, (and certainly, *out*), gay man.

We get into trouble when we continue to impart god-like qualities to our parents—including immortality. Many people still defer to their parents for guidance years after their deaths. We do so when we haven't really left home yet—figuratively speaking. We may have moved a thousand miles away, but emotionally, we're still living under Mom and Dad's roof/influence. "With nothing and no one to judge them against, we assume them to be perfect parents. As our world broadens beyond our crib, we develop a need to maintain this image of perfection as a defense against the great unknowns we increasingly encounter. As long as we believe our parents are perfect, we feel protected" (Forward, p. 16).

Although leaving home requires an actual physical disconnection for an indefinite period of time (in extreme cases, possibly a complete severing of the relationship which we will talk about later); it is about so much more than just getting a new address. In fact, merely moving across the country, or to the other side of the world, for that matter, doesn't necessarily mean that person has ever left home in the way that we're talking about.

If the gay man continues to see his parents as the two most important people in his world, he will remain uninitiated. If he continues to defer to them *first* when making important decisions, if he's not out to them, if he's still giving them his power and keeping huge pieces of his life a secret from them, all those miles don't mean anything. Leaving home is synonymous with *individuation* and a gay man's ability to be a Warrior can be directly assessed based on how successfully he has *individuated* from his family.

For the gay man, separating from his family of origin can be more difficult than for the straight person. For the latter, there is something about sameness that can facilitate separation. *I am like them, and in that very likeness, I have some understanding of their approval of me; therefore, I can go out in the world and be my own person knowing that I have these people back there who support me, if for no other reason, my heterosexuality.*

The gay man often has no such understanding. His differentness may serve as an impetus for staying connected rather than for separating. He may, in subtle and unconscious ways, remain connected to his parents in hopes of someday hearing what he has longed to hear for so long: *Son, we approve of you just as you are.* If he does not receive this message of approval from them, he may continue going back to this dry well, each time hoping for a different result.

Most often the result is the same; but nevertheless, this futile quest keeps him emotionally and psychically tied to his family. The energy that he could be using to find people who could indeed support and approve of him is instead wasted on staying connected to a fantasy. If we have parents who don't approve of us or don't like us, but we stay connected to the fantasy that they are benevolent and well-intentioned people, we will never be able to move through our world as strong, powerful gay men. Instead, we will be emotionally crippled "boys" with self-esteem in the red.

ROAD BLOCKS

Of the many roadblocks that hinder a gay man's ability to healthily separate from his family, there is one that stands above the rest. It is based on the Judeo-Christian tenet: *Honor thy father and thy mother* (read: *under any and all circumstances*). This teaching, on the surface, appears benevolent enough. But when it is overlaid on a dysfunctional/unsupportive family system, it can take on a very skewed meaning for the gay man.

Alice Miller's book, *For Your Own Good,* discusses child-rearing practices in Germany over the last several hundred years. She spotlights the upbringing of Adolf Hitler to exemplify her point, that in the name of honoring the father and the mother, great atrocities can be committed. She calls this the *poisonous pedagogy*. She explains that it is wrong to impart "false information and beliefs that have been passed on from generation to generation and dutifully accepted by the young even though they are not only unproven but are demonstrably false" (p. 59). Other examples include: obedience makes a child strong; a high degree of self-esteem is harmful; tenderness (doting) is harmful; a feeling of duty produces love; strong feelings are harmful; and parents are always right.

Research shows that children who are abused often show unwarranted loyalty to the abusive parent. A child who is abused learns to transfer his anger in time onto other (safer) targets in order to maintain his sense of allegiance to his parents, no matter how abusive they may have been. In the case of Hitler, he turned the unconscious anger that he carried toward his extremely abusive father and weak mother onto a group of people that he believed deserved his wrath.

In the case of gay men, one client's story illustrates this problem. Greg was a 38-year-old attorney, a practicing alcoholic, who had been in a number of short-term relationships, each ending in disaster. He began therapy to figure out why all of his primary relationships had failed.

Greg's father, also an alcoholic, had never allowed Greg to bring any of his partners to their home. Nevertheless, he went "home" for every holiday and even for his parent's 50th anniversary. His mother asked that he understand his family's position; and additionally, she felt he should not flaunt his "lifestyle." He continued to send birthday presents to all the family members and to do favors for them, even lending his brother $3,000.00 for a down payment on a boat (the same brother who would not spend the night in his house for fear of contracting AIDS, even though Greg was HIV negative).

No one in the family ever acknowledged *his* birthday and of course, never mentioned his partners. But Greg consistently refused to consider leaving this poisonous environment. He could identify the extreme physical abuse that the entire family had received from his alcoholic father and understand that his mother did nothing to protect him or his siblings. He also saw how his mother played him and his siblings against each other and how withholding of love she had been.

Unfortunately, he could not make the leap to understanding how the abuse and abandonment continued into the present. Nor could he understand why three partners had left him, since, as he believed, he was such a loving and caring person.

In fact, Greg carried an enormous amount of anger and rage, but was unable to express any of it to the people who really deserved it. Instead, periodically he would unload these feelings on the current partner creating an atmosphere of unsafety and mistrust. After enough of these explosive rampages, Greg would once again find himself alone.

Although it might be easy to understand anyone's reluctance to leave his family, the consequences of remaining in one such as Greg's, are life-threatening—as life -threatening as any addiction. Until Greg was able to realize this, he would remain alone and unhappy. Individuation from one's family is very hard work and frightens many people into complacency.

THE CHALLENGES OF
LEAVING AN EXTENDED FAMILY

Special attention needs to be given to the challenges a gay man will face in leaving home when he has grown up in an extended family. Some examples of this would include those who live in small towns where there is a strong loyalty to one's ethnic group, or in specific neighborhoods where many members of the extended family have remained, and where the ethnic culture emphasizes continued membership in the family over independence and individuation from them.

Although such cultural conditioning that discourages separation can be found within Anglo culture, it does not appear to be as prevalent as in the Hispanic or Asian communities, or with other people of color. Within the Hispanic world, for instance, there is a cultural expectation that a grown man will continue to live with his family until he marries. This unspoken "rule," or custom, is often built into the social fabric of certain ethic groups and is certainly not exclusive to the Hispanic world.

From a sociological perspective, this custom can be economical, cultural, or psychological. We need not concern our exploration with the economical reasons for an adult remaining in his parents' home; at times there is no other alternative. But it is important here to examine the cultural and psychological reasons. Because something is part of a culture, it is not necessarily healthy. Just as with Anglos, many Latin men remain "little boys" well into their adulthood, and even though it is customary for these men to remain in their parents' home, it is important that they examine whether it is serving them in becoming adults. The blind allegiance some Latin men have toward their parents can be disastrous.

For the gay man who experiences such a custom, it can be especially problematic. In Mexico and most other Spanish-speaking countries, it is not unusual to find a gay man living at home well into his 50's. He may have an active sex life outside the home, but he will continue to follow the cultural expectation that he live with his parents since he is not married.

Clearly this custom can be found within many cultures around the world, although a far cry from the nuclear family model of many Anglo families in the United States, and must therefore be considered in the larger picture of Initiation. Certainly, living in an extended family can be a rich and meaningful part of one's life—helping the individual to feel a sense of belonging and a "place" within his world. But such a situation can only work if it embraces the full diversity and uniqueness of each of the members.

James Hillman says that we were never expected to live this way, in other words, we were never expected to live in nuclear families the way we do in much of present society: mother, father and one or two children. From an historical perspective, it seems like we were meant to live in extended families, where the burden of responsibilities is shared among a number of adults, and children are exposed to a multitude of roles: aunts, uncles, cousins, grandparents. In this way, the trials and tribulations of life are experienced collectively and can be less stressful than they are in the nuclear family.

When the extended family is accepting of the gay man's sexuality, the support available to him can be extraordinary. With such support, he has a place in the cosmos—a rare occurrence for many gay men. He does not have to hide who he is and he can know he is loved and accepted regardless of his sexuality.

We know of a few situations like this from men we've worked with here in Santa Fe. Carlos comes from a large Hispanic family in Northern New Mexico. During family gatherings, he and his partner, Bill, are as welcomed as his married siblings. Bill is considered part of the family. They both attend graduations, birthday parties, weddings, and funerals. They have a support system to rely on when they need it.

Carlos' mother has told him that she feels Bill is an additional son, and Bill (an accountant) helps Carlos' father with his taxes. On several occasions, Bill has even taken Carlos' grandmother to doctors' appointments. Clearly, within this family system, there is a place for Carlos and Bill. They are treated with the equal respect and dignity as offered their straight siblings and spouses, and their relationship is considered to be as real and viable as anyone else's within their family.

However, such experiences of acceptance within an extended family are not always the case for gay men. In fact, because of the importance placed on the *continuation of family* within most ethnic groups, a gay man within such a group may find specific challenges and obstacles to his Initiation. Gay men who have grown up in an extended family environment might find it more difficult to separate from their families because of cultural rules and expectations. These expectations may include homophobic attitudes, a need for him to marry and deny his sexual orientation, and loyalty to a religious organization that judges him unacceptable.

Often, certain members within a gay man's extended family may be less than accepting of his sexuality; such lack of acceptance may be either overt (obvious) or covert (subtle and indirect). In this situation, the gay man may be forced to live in denial and secrecy. If he is out to his family, he then runs the risk of being subjected to rejection and/or overt hostility where there is little understanding shown for his differentness.

It is even worse when the hostility remains covert and unspoken, for then the toxicity may be more insidious and harder to identify. When this is the case, when all or part of the extended family refuses to accept his homosexuality, the only healthy choice he has is to set very firm boundaries and, if necessary, to separate from those who cannot accept him. This is an extremely important issue and warrants further exploration.

If a gay man continues to remain in a toxic environment (where he is blatantly and unequivocally rejected for his sexuality), he will be adversely affected in deep and long-lasting ways. His self-worth and identity may be severely damaged. He must understand that a toxic environment is exactly that—one that is poisoning him and may eventually include life-threatening consequences, such as: drug addiction; HIV infection (if it happens out of self-loathing or from an unconscious death wish); or some other type of physical disease or emotional imbalance, that can eventually lead to soul death, if not physical death.

If his family environment is poisoning him, as difficult as it may be, he must leave. In contemplating this option, he may ask: *What do I have left without my family? Where is my safety net? Will anyone else really be there for me?* Often such questions, if left unanswered, can lead him into confusion and despair. But until he finds meaningful answers to these questions, he will remain tied to his toxic family for years, unable to figure out why his life is such a mess. At some point, he must engage in an initiation process that will help him move away from this toxicity and find replacements that are life-enhancing and congruent with whom he is attempting to become. This could be therapy, 12-step work, or a process of establishing another community that will accept him completely.

Our friend and colleague, Randy Gunnoe, had one such client whom we will call Dang. Dang was an Asian man from a very large family in the Bay Area. Dang had AIDS and while the family was aware of his physical condition, they offered him little compassion. He was the second from the youngest of nine children. Most of the siblings had antagonistic relationships with each other. His mother had died several years before and his father was 91 years old and in poor health. Even though his father had been severely abusive to all of the family, Dang felt that it was his duty to make sure his father was cared for. He spent all of his spare time with his father and stayed several days a week with him, even though this was a great hardship, requiring a cross-town commute and long periods of time away from his partner.

He could not understand why his brothers and sisters were not willing to spend more time in caring for their father. He resisted the notion that, since his father had been so abusive, it was possible that they were not interested in helping. Furthermore, he could not understand that they might have felt that they didn't have to do anything, since he was willing to do most of the work. He resisted the suggestion that if he stopped doing so much, his siblings would pick up the slack. In good codependent fashion, he believed that if he didn't do it, no one would; and even if they did, it wouldn't be good enough. It is important to understand that these were merely Dang's perceptions of his family's unwillingness to help.

Any suggestion proffered was met with resistance. Dang was determined to sacrifice his well being for that of his father's. Dang's partner was becoming increasingly angrier as he felt more and more neglected. He could not understand why Dang continued to put his father's needs above all else.

In Dang's therapy, he could acknowledge his father's continual abusive behavior, but would become angry if it was suggested that he was putting his father's needs before his own and his partner's. He felt guilty whenever he stayed away for more than a few days and was terrified at the prospect of his father's death.

There are many issues that could be examined here: the dysfunction of the family, alienation, codependency, self-esteem, guilt, abuse and extreme dependency. But the issue at hand was Dang's inability to free himself from his destructive family. The consequences of his inability to leave home were profound. His partner eventually left him and Dang died from an AIDS-related illness, almost a year before his father did.

KNOWING WHEN AND HOW TO LEAVE

If a gay man is living in a toxic family environment, and he comes to understand that he must leave this environment in order to be healthy, it is important that he does not just suddenly walk away. Our client, Humberto, did just that. He realized that he was slowly drowning in the hostility he experienced from his family and had to get away from their toxicity, so he fled to a large city on the west coast.

Unfortunately, he knew no one there and had absolutely no support system to take the place of his large family. He floundered and eventually returned to his hometown. He then felt that he had no options because he had failed so miserably to establish a replacement for his family. We might say that Humberto had, unconsciously, set himself up for failure. He needed to do the work that would have enabled him to create a new support system. *And he needed to grieve the loss of his family.*

Humberto came back from the large city with AIDS. His family allowed him to come home, but they would not allow him to tell anyone about his situation. Even though he was living in the same house, his father would not speak to him. Humberto died eight months after returning home. At his funeral neither his disease nor his sexuality were mentioned. His family and the church did not support a huge part of this man's identity. His mother would not allow his friends to say anything about his sexual orientation nor their relationship with her son at the graveside service. Humberto died and was buried without his identity.

When a gay man realizes that he can no longer live with the toxicity of an un-accepting family, he must acknowledge this tremendous loss. He must be willing to go through the process of grieving in the same way he would if someone had died. In reality, something has died, not only his relationship with his family, but in this case, the fantasy he has clung to—the fantasy that he had a loving, supportive family.

Such grieving is exceedingly hard work and the gay man in this situation needs all the support he can get. There is a good possibility that he may never have had the love and support he thought he had, and he may only now be able to acknowledge the truth of his situation. Nevertheless, it will take time to heal the wounds that this type of abandonment produces.

Some people may believe that the gay man is better off staying a part of the family, even if his sexuality is not accepted. Some families will maintain that their gay children are still loved, even though their sexuality is not acknowledged. These are the families that say, "You will always be our son and we love you, but we don't need to talk about it. And we would rather that you not bring your boyfriend home with you."

Such beliefs are a part of the toxic system. They negate the gay man's essence and strip him of his dignity. These beliefs are also what fuel a gay man's addictions. If he cannot acknowledge the truth about his family, he may need something to "help" him stay in the denial or the fantasy. Better to drink or get stoned or work or have sex or shop, than acknowledge the pain of having a family that will not love him. Additionally, he may rage at innocent people in his life, those (like his friends or his partner) who have nothing to do with the rejection he feels from his family.

If the gay man is unsuccessful in changing the toxic environment of his family, he must realize that he can no longer remain imprisoned in the fantasy "that he is loved." He must acknowledge the damage that is being done to him in the name of love. His self-esteem is being stripped from him and he must consciously become aware of the extreme sacrifice he is being asked to make to remain a part of his family.

Encouraging gay men to leave toxic environments is sometimes met with great resistance. They will cling to the belief that leaving the family is too great a step to take toward greater self-esteem. They will explore every other avenue in order to "fix" the problem, constantly avoiding the real issue. They will blame their friends for not being available enough, their partners for not loving them enough, and their bosses for not valuing them enough. All the while the "elephant in the living room" will be their lack of family support. We have worked with many such individuals, who constantly repeat the refrain, "I just don't know, I just don't know. I've tried everything and nothing works." But they are terrified to look at the most important issue, the issue that is causing the problem—their unaccepting family.

Leaving home is necessary for our Initiation, and thus individuation; however, it is not the end of the journey. The destination of this journey is, at some point, to re-enter the family—now as an adult. This is the *incorporation* phase of Initiation. Unfortunately, this phase does not occur if the family remains toxic. In order for *incorporation* to be possible, the family must be willing to see this person as an equal, with his own set of beliefs and values, and his own power.

HEALING THE INNER HOMOPHOBE

Me, Homophobic?

If, in short, the gay subculture sometimes seems almost to be its own worst enemy, perhaps it is because so many of the people in it are suffering from a self-hatred so deep that they can't even begin to acknowledge it to themselves.

...people are very sensitive to your own sense of self-worth, to your own self-image. If you feel ashamed or afraid, regardless of whether you overtly show it, they can sense those feelings. People will inevitably treat you as you feel you should be treated. If you don't respect your self, if you don't trust yourself, you will never be able to inspire that trust and respect in those around you.
— from *A Place at the Table*, Bruce Bawer, pp. 183 and 242.

The next step in a gay man's Initiation is to heal his Inner Homophobe. Internalized homophobia is about rejection, intense dislike, or even hatred of one's own gayness at a core level. A gay man's ability to love himself is directly proportional to the degree to which he has successfully identified, and worked to heal, his own internalized homophobia. Internalized homophobia is a natural outcome of living in a world that continues to project its fear, lack of acceptance and harsh judgment onto gay people.

Take, for example, the extreme homophobic doctrine or tradition found within most organized religions. If a gay man is a Christian fundamentalist, an Orthodox Jew, a Mormon, or member of any other church that holds a blatant anti-gay position, he will be bombarded with homophobic messages regularly, reminding him that his sexuality is wrong, sinful, an abomination, which may in turn reinforce his internalized homophobia. A case in point can be found in the anti-gay reformation taking place currently within the Roman Catholic church. In response to the ever-increasing sexual abuse cases, some prominent Catholic leaders decided to target gay priests and link them to pedophilia. Why? Research shows that the overriding majority of pedophiles are heterosexual. What is the message being sent within the church, not only to gay priests but to gay parishioners as well? *We do not accept you.*

Likewise, if a gay man is in the military, he will often be confronted with homophobic policies and rules. He learns through obeying the "Don't Ask Don't Tell" rule that he must live in secrecy and carry some degree of shame about who he is.

Whenever we remain members of organizations or families that tell us we are wrong or unacceptable or that require us to hide because we are gay, we cannot help but internalize, to some degree, their homophobia of us. Leaving abusive organizations can be as important as leaving abusive families.

Within each gay person there exists a dimension that we call the Inner Homophobe—that part of us that does not like being gay, that might even *hate* being gay. Until we get in touch with the Inner Homophobe, we have no chance of healing it. We will not understand how this self-hatred can influence our perceptions of ourselves and of our world, and affect the decisions we make from one moment to the next.

When we see a new client, we often ask how he feels about being gay. Even though the responses vary, one thing appears to be consistent: The question creates some level of cognitive dissonance; it seems to throw the client off just a bit. In answering, most men will say something like: "I feel good about being gay," accompanied by a look that might convey more than just those words: "I'm a gay man...Aren't I supposed to say that I feel good about being gay?"

Very few clients, in the beginning, talk about their internalized homophobia. It's usually not until the client begins to feel a sense of trust, that he allows himself to go deeper into the significance of the question regarding his homophobia. Then he can respond from a deeper place of knowing, which will include his past wounding and trauma related to his gayness.

It is not that the first answer is necessarily wrong or untruthful, but there is more to the truth than just "I feel fine about being gay." Most of us have been too injured to *only* feel fine about our sexuality. The first response may be due in part to a client wanting to make a good impression, but we believe it's more than that. It also points to the gay man's resistance to acknowledge his wounding.

A type of magical thinking can fuel this resistance: *if I don't talk about it, it can't hurt me.* And further: *If I talk about my shadow feelings (i.e. dislike, ambivalence, hatred) concerning my gayness, then I might give those feelings power.* But as expected of magical thinking, it is incorrect.

Talking about self-hatred, and feeling the pain associated with it, will not reinforce it; instead such work can provide us with a way out of the labyrinth of internalized homophobia. In fact, what really fuels our self-hatred is not talking about it and pretending that it doesn't exist. The awareness of our self-loathing behaviors, attitudes and unconscious motivations brings us our salvation. It is the path to authentic self-love.

When we begin to acknowledge and talk about any aspect of ourselves, and in particular a shadow aspect, the more chance we will have to heal that piece. That is, if we want to figure out how to love ourselves more, we have to first recognize the ways in which we don't love ourselves and start from there. It's a simple rule of psychology: *That which we don't own, we act out.* If we don't own (i.e. acknowledge, talk about and feel) our self-hatred, it will manifest in all sorts of bizarre and counter-productive ways.

The Inner Homophobe is a characteristic present within all gay men. No gay person living in Western society today is exempt—no matter how great and loving his childhood was. Our society is simply too homophobic for us to have made it into adulthood without internalizing some degree of that hatred.

The Inner Homophobe, along with carrying our self-hatred, also possesses all the shame and judgment from those who have told us that we are wrong, sinful, mistakes, that we are against the will of God, the work of the devil, and on and on. The Inner Homophobe carries the memories of being beaten up because of his gayness, shunned by his peer group, or made to be the brunt of shameful and dishonoring "queer jokes." Maybe he remembers Dad making fun of some effeminate man he saw walking by, referring to him as a "fruit." Whatever the memory, the feelings of shame and judgment may still be alive and active within.

The Inner Homophobe is one of the most important components of a gay man's shadow. Unless he understands this, he will remain oblivious to how powerful this shadow can be in determining his day-to-day interactions, his perceptions of himself and his world, and his ability (or more precisely, inability) to love himself in a genuine and sustainable manner.

When we recognize our internalized homophobia, we stop pretending that we are completely healed from the severe wounding that we incurred over years of persecution at school, in the community, and/or at home. Until then, we run the risk of letting the Inner Homophobe make certain important decisions, keeping us victims, leading us into isolation, loneliness and despair.

If we consider for a moment how many negative messages a gay man is subjected to within a year, or even a month, of his life, it makes sense that he would internalize some of this oppression and bigotry. He might begin to believe, on an unconscious level, that he is a second-class citizen, and not deserving of equal rights and the same protections offered straight people. He might also believe that it is acceptable that his primary relationships be invalidated by society.

Internalized homophobia may appear in obvious ways: through self-destructive behavior, addiction, self-sabotaging thoughts, low self-esteem, feeling ashamed of who one is or of what one does. At other times, it takes on a more subtle and insidious form.

■   ■   ■

Conrad and his partner, Grant, had been contemplating adoption for several years. After many discussions about this issue, where Grant would express excitement and readiness at the prospect of expanding their family, Conrad remained ambivalent and confused. Finally, Conrad decided to enter therapy in hopes of better understanding what was preventing him from making a decision.

During the first session, Conrad began talking about the coming-out incident with his mother, which had happened eight years after he and Grant had gotten together. He recounted how she struggled with the information and went through some of the usual parental responses: guilt, sadness, wondering if it was her fault, or if it was because Conrad's father had been so unavailable.

This incident had been playing on his mind recently, and for reasons he could not explain, he had dreamed about it several nights before. He remembered her look of abject disdain as she stood before him holding a locked box.

Conrad said with a sad tone, "My mother asked me to promise her something. I took this to mean she was coming around to the idea of my being gay and wanted some kind of better understanding of this whole issue of my sexuality. And then to my total amazement, she said, 'Promise me that you and Grant will never have children.' I was shocked."

Conrad felt a tremendous sense of betrayal at the time, but knew he must have suppressed those feelings in order to continue the discussion. He added, "I guess I put those feelings in a box and locked it shut. Maybe that's what's happening now, and what the dream was about. I'm trying to figure out how my mother's words affected me." We continued:

"How do you think you felt?"

"Totally enraged."

"What did you do with that rage?"

"I don't know. (some moments of silence) I guess I turned it in on myself—once again."

"How so?"

"Maybe I let her request influence my decision-making more than I realized?

"The request that you and Grant not have children?"

"Yeah, that one. Because once again she was telling me that I was not okay. No, not just not okay—totally unacceptable. And in this case, that I wasn't fit to be a parent. Maybe I took it to heart."

"It sounds like you're identifying some kind of unconscious allegiance you've had to your mother that you're beginning to understand on a more conscious level. Tell me more."

"I think I've been placing her needs before my own and letting her blatant homophobia influence more of my decisions than I ever realized. Like my ambivalence about having kids. So much of it seems to go back to that discussion I had with her a long time ago."

"Conrad, do you think that what your mother said to you was abusive?"

"Before today, I would have probably said no. But now, after talking about it with you, I'm beginning to see not only the abuse, but how it has reinforced my own internalized homophobia. Man, this is pretty intense."

"So how does this affect your feelings about adopting children?"

"I guess my challenge now is to figure out how much *not* wanting kids was my unconscious allegiance to my mother's homophobia."

"Yes, and the next challenge would be to figure out how much of your desire to have children is in reaction to your mother, rather than coming from an authentic need within yourself."

"Wow, that's big..."

■ ■ ■

Just *feeling fine* about being gay gives no acknowledgment of the Inner Homophobe—that part of ourselves that has been damaged by the years of discrimination, assault, and psychic violence waged against each of us.

Always, an oppressed person's greatest challenge is in healing the internalized oppression. It is that place within him that has come to believe that he is not as valuable, not as deserving, or that he is completely loathsome. In having had to traverse those minefields, how could we come out of such a battle unscathed? As gay adults, we are left with deep and often unhealed wounds, where the sediment of hatred and deprecation still reside.

Conrad was beginning to discover his particular version of the Inner Homophobe. Finding it was a blessing—not a curse. Once we understand how we dislike or even hate our gayness, and where those feelings originate, we can begin to see how subtle and pervasive such self-hatred can be, and how it undermines our true desires and prevents us from loving ourselves. With that awareness, we can begin a process of deep inner healing.

THERAPY

A Contemporary Form of Initiation

Surrender has introduced me to a new type of warriorship and new meanings for fear and courage. I invoke courage in my life by honoring and welcoming fully the extent of my fear. Recovery seems to be about facing fear. Every decision to confront the unfaceable— entering therapy, willingly exposing the raw places of my psyche, this is warriorship. I have even begun to celebrate fear. Courage is not about *not* being afraid. It is about welcoming the fact that I fear.
— *To Hell and Back: One Man's Recovery*, Tav Sparks, p. 92.

Psychotherapy is a contemporary form of Initiation. When successful, it can be one of Western culture's best replacements for an initiative process that would be found more naturally in indigenous cultures. Therapy, as with any effective initiative process, can and should help a person move from a place of adolescence to adulthood. In its purest form, therapy contains all three elements of successful Initiation: *separation, transition and incorporation.*

Therapy teaches the client about *separation.* Effective therapy helps the client begin to identify how he may continue to be unhealthily connected to his family of origin, to locate the areas within his psyche that are not yet individuated from his parents. In exploring the relationship to his family of origin, the client may begin to see some problem areas—namely how his emotional ties to his parents may be keeping him boy-like and unable to live as a strong man. In time, the individual accomplishes a symbolic separation from the web of childhood fantasies.

Therapy helps people break away from the structure of their families in order to find a separate set of values and philosophy. As we have already stressed, most families in our society do not encourage adult children to individuate; rather they teach obedience, loyalty and allegiance to them *over all other relationships.* Such teachings wreak havoc in an adult's life, for they prevent him from having truly adult relationships.

Individuation is the process by which one separates from his family, by cutting the psychic umbilical cord and forming his own identity, a unique sense of self—separate from his mother and father. Children are extensions of their parents. Teenagers, on the other hand, often react in opposition to this extension, but it is done within the parameters of the family system. *I don't want to follow your rules, but I still need you to take care of me.* Healthy adults are neither extensions nor reactions to their parents, but rather freethinking, autonomous people.

The therapeutic experience is a process of change; therefore it also contains a *transition* phase. It is a journey that can be, at times, both painful and frightening, taking the client into increasingly deeper levels of consciousness. It requires courage and strength to navigate this hazardous terrain. Scott Peck says, "Those who come to psychotherapy are the wisest and most courageous among us…only the wiser and braver among us…are willing to submit to the difficult process of self-examination that happens in a psychotherapist's office."

Lastly, psychotherapy includes the third phase of Initiation, *incorporation*. Therapy helps the client to incorporate his newfound awareness and individuation into the world he left behind. He is now able to relate to his family as an adult. The purpose of individuation is not to completely sever one's relationship to family of origin (*except in those instances when the family remains toxic*), but rather to help the client learn how to interact with his family more honestly and on the level of adult to adult.

Therapy helps the client to return—with more honesty and compassion—to his family, friends, and the community at large. This reintegration, now as a self-actualized adult, is the ultimate purpose of Initiation. Therapy helps the individual to relate to his world more responsibly; to move away from the childhood wounding that has kept him floundering in the abyss of childish fears.

Although we are referring specifically to adults and how therapy helps to initiate them, the same holds true for adolescents. Jay Haley, *Uncommon Therapy*, explains that therapy also helps the adolescent with Initiation. "For many adolescents, help from a professional therapist becomes an initiation ceremony, in that it provides a relationship with an outsider whose goal is to help him achieve independence and maturity" (p.47).

GETTING IN TOUCH WITH FEELINGS

What remains true for everyone is that to diminish one's capacity to experience pain is to diminish one's capacity to experience pleasure.
— *Taking Back the Disowned Self*, Nathaniel Branden, p. 282.

We don't *meditate* them [feelings] away or "transcend" them or "turn them over" before we've experienced them.
— *Recovery: Plain and Simple*, John Lee, p. 73.

One of the main goals of any initiative journey is to help a person come to a deeper understanding of himself. Psychotherapy accomplishes this goal by helping the client get in touch with his feelings. Feelings are our guides that lead us into the deeper realms of the psyche. They are an integral part of each person's intelligence. The intellect alone is not enough to help us find our way through the labyrinth of life; without a connection to our feelings, we become spiritually adrift.

Feelings connect our conscious minds to our souls. They direct us to the places within the body, mind, and soul where there is still more work to be done. As well, our feelings are our radar. Without our emotional radar working, we have a greater chance of running aground or crashing into something or someone. Our feelings tell us about the nuances of our world.

All feelings have a specific function. For instance, fear tells us about potential danger. Guilt tells us that we have done something wrong and helps us to take responsibility for our actions. Happiness allows us to find a sense of well being. It reminds us of the beauty of life.

In using therapy as an initiative process, the two most important feelings to explore are: sadness and anger. Sadness is the cleansing feeling. It helps us to locate where our grief and unhealed trauma reside. Sadness is the psyche's way of releasing and resolving grief and it provides us with the ability to manage loss. Often a "good cry" is followed by a sense of relief/release. Crying helps us to lighten our psychic load. There is a sense of discharge; energy has moved through and out of us.

While grief allows us to heal and reconnect with the world, anger serves an equally important purpose. Its function is to help protect us. It might be the result of our needs being in conflict with someone else's or of a boundary violation. It allows us to say to our world, "You may not treat me this way!" Or, "I will not allow you to disrespect/abuse me!" Or, even stronger, "How dare you try to hurt me like this!" Without healthy anger, we cannot protect ourselves. With too much anger, we run the risk of alienating those in our world and ending up alone.

In the therapy office, a client's anger is a trickier emotion for a therapist to deal with than the other emotions. It takes greater skill as a therapist to ride the rapids with the client in his anger—in all its intensity, uncertainty and power—than it does to comfort him and provide a nurturing space for him in his sadness.

A therapist can only take a client as deep into his anger as the therapist has been willing to venture within himself. Some therapists avoid anger at all cost. They may do so by using a particular style that leaves little room for the client to ever deal with his anger.

A colleague once told us, "I'm not interested in people's anger." We were incredulous. How can you help people to heal, if you can't allow them to get in touch with their anger? Why should anger be any less real than sadness, or any other emotion? This particular therapist was masterful with his technique, but his clients were never given permission to be angry, whether it was at him or their parents or the world in general.

In cases like this, there may be an unspoken contract from the beginning of the therapy that the therapist conveys, either overtly or otherwise: *Thou shalt not be angry here.* If the therapist gives the message that anger is not permitted (whether it is through humor, by being a nice guy, or overly nurturing), the client will be deprived of one of the greatest therapeutic opportunities—to use anger as an initiative tool.

We believe that the majority of gay men carry a lot of anger—and rightfully so. Most of us, from an early age, were the target of other people's hatred and oppression. Throughout our lives, our rights have been violated, our needs often ignored. As children, many of us were humiliated and shamed because of our differentness. Considering such experiences, it makes sense that we would still be angry about the abuse that we have experienced.

A surprising number of gay clients report, especially in the beginning of their work, that they don't feel much anger. What happened to it? Where did it go? Some gay men tend to believe that once they come out, they can let go of all experiences of shaming, victimization and oppression. *Now that I'm out—and free—I don't need to be angry any longer.* It is understandable that we would want to let go of the pain that we carried for so many years as outcasts. But unless we are willing to revisit that pain, which usually includes a vast reservoir of anger, we will be destined to act out that unresolved anger in unconscious and detrimental ways.

Many gay men are unaware that they might be sitting on an emotional powder keg that could blow at any time, given the right (or wrong?) set of circumstances. Often these men vent their anger in passive, indirect ways. Sometimes their anger appears in the form of bitchy, campy humor. Other times, it might take on a more self-destructive tone, as addictions or unsafe sex. Whatever the style that we've chosen, until we find where our anger resides, we will be motivated by it unconsciously.

■　■　■

Psychotherapy offers the client a journey of Initiation. Initiation is as much about recognizing anger as it is sadness or any other emotion associated with the healing process. In order to be an effective form of Initiation, psychotherapy should help gay men get in touch with *all* their feelings. This can help them learn to give those feelings a voice and to move emotional energy out of their bodies, so that they can begin to get free of the energy that would otherwise continue to weigh them down and keep them stuck.

When the client is finished with the initiative journey of psychotherapy, he is fundamentally and irrevocably changed. He will often see himself as a different person —someone new. He may even look physically different from when he started the work. He will have learned a new language—the language of Adulthood.

PART V

THE GAY WARRIOR

The term Gay Warrior describes a man who has successfully matured and completed a journey of Initiation in which he has *consciously* individuated from his family of origin, *consciously* grown out of his *Puer*, and *consciously* worked to transform his betrayals into wisdom. There is no one template that would characterize the Gay Warrior. That is, there may be many variations on this theme. However, each of us, when we find our own unique version of the Warrior, will possess some common elements of adulthood, freedom and responsibility to self and our community.

Here, we explore the most important characteristics of the Gay Warrior; we begin by looking at Warrior characteristics within gay relationship, and then explore politics, work, aging, and finally, spirituality. Our intention is to create a road map of sorts for gay men to reference when they find themselves in uncharted territory. There are no absolutes on how to be a Warrior, but the more we speak our truth, the closer we get to finding this essential energy force within, and the better we become at discerning what is Warrior behavior and what's not.

This road map is a compilation of our years of work with many gay men who have been in search of their own Warrior. Primarily, this information comes from literally hundreds of group therapy sessions we've facilitated since we began this work in the late 80's. As well, we have drawn from our years together as a couple, and have attempted to offer the reader a glimpse of our process—one which has been far from perfect, with our share of crises, as well as triumphs. But always without a road map—one that, had it existed, would have shown the arduous journey of men before us, pointing out the major pit falls and roadblocks along the way as well as scenic byways. Use what works and leave the rest. It's a roadmap that has worked for us: yours might be a little different.

THE WARRIOR RELATIONSHIP

When a gay man is living as a Warrior, he has a much greater ability to be in an intimate and long-term relationship with another man. This is not to say, however, that being in a relationship is synonymous with being initiated. There are many gay men in relationships, even long-term ones, who have done very little initiation work. Conversely, there are those men who have already done a lot of initiation work who show strong Warrior qualities, who are not currently in a relationship.

As mentioned earlier, there are other archetypes of the mature masculine that constitute the full-fledged adult man: the King, the Magician and the Lover. It seems only natural to include in an examination of Gay Relationship a mention of the Lover archetype.

"The Lover is the archetype of play and of 'display,' of healthy embodiment, of being in the world of sensuous pleasure and in one's own body *without shame*. Thus, the Lover is *deeply sensual*— sensually aware and sensitive to the physical world in all its splendor." (Moore and Gillette, p. 121).

Clearly, gay men tend to have a more well-developed Lover archetype than Warrior. Not surprisingly, most gay fiction, as well as gay film, focuses heavily on the Lover archetype.

However, having a strong connection to one's Lover archetype does not necessarily ensure that a gay man will experience success in relationship. Obviously something more is needed. Gay men must also have a well-developed Warrior to find depth and fullness in a relationship. Since it's easier for most gay men to access their Lover than their Warrior, we have deliberately concentrated, in this chapter and throughout the book, on the archetype that most gay men have not developed as well—the Warrior. With this said, the first questions to explore concerning gay relationship and becoming a Warrior are:

If you *are* in a relationship:
    With what I now know about Initiation, am I functioning

as an initiated gay man in this relationship? Am I living as a Warrior within myself and with this man?

If you *are not* in a relationship:
With what I now know about Initiation, am I ready for a mature relationship with another man? When the next relationship opportunity presents itself, will I be able to respond as a Warrior?

The concept of two men in a love relationship, living and growing together can often generate different feelings depending on the person. Excitement and longing for the young man newly-out who wants more than anything to connect and develop intimacy with another man; for the one who has never found it, sadness and despair; and perhaps, for those who have, a sense of satisfaction and peace.

Even today, a healthy gay relationship continues to be somewhat of an anomaly. Certainly, there should be more given the number of gay men in search of them. Especially rare seem to be the long-term relationships where, after twenty, or even ten years, both partners continue to feel emotionally satisfied, sexually turned on by each other, and intellectually and spiritually stimulated.

Healthy gay relationships are possible and they do exist; although there aren't as many of them as there could be in proportion to the number of men looking for them. In observing this aspect of the gay experience, we began to ask ourselves these questions. Why do most gay relationships last less than two years? Why aren't there more healthy ones? What's preventing gay men from finding more depth and longevity with a partner?

As therapists, we have considered these questions from a psychological and sociological perspective. As a gay couple, with many years of relationship experience, we've looked at them from a personal and relational perspective. There are a number of factors related to the disproportionately small number of healthy gay relationships. These factors include:

- The lack of Initiated gay men
- The newness of being in visibly "out" gay relationships
- The impact of the AIDS epidemic
- The lack of appropriate gay relationship models
- The impact of marriage
- Sex addiction

- Separating friendship from love
- The power of the *Puer*
- The avoidance of conflict

First, and most important, a gay man must have experienced an Initiation process in order to have a successful love relationship. Until a gay man has done his separation work from his family of origin, he will have little chance of finding a healthy, long-term relationship. As long as his emotional and psychic allegiance remains to his parents, his partner won't stand a chance.

When Mom and Dad continue to come first, his primary relationship will be to them. One example of him putting them first is going "home" for the holidays and not taking his partner with him because he does not want to hurt their feelings or they don't approve of his "friend." Another example is his deferring to them when making important decisions. Whatever the specifics, if his relationship to his partner continues to be relegated to secondary status, such a condition will negatively effect every aspect of that relationship, and in time erode its foundation.

■ ■ ■

Gay men, as a distinct and separate social group, are a relatively new phenomenon. Only in the last thirty years, since Stonewall, have we finally succeeded in forming a collective identity of ourselves; this is not much time in the big scheme of things. Sociologically speaking, gay men are still in their adolescence.

In the '70s, the primary focus of the gay community was coming out. Then the focus shifted quickly to the AIDS epidemic and consumed a lot of our time for the next twenty years. Only recently have gay men been able to rechannel their energy and begin to figure out how to make relationships work over the long run. Even though men have been exploring relationships with other men since the beginning of time, only in the last 30 years have we been able to do so without the fear of being tortured, imprisoned and/or murdered en masse. It behooves us to remember that we are navigating new and uncharted waters.

■ ■ ■

The AIDS epidemic has profoundly affected gay men's perceptions and experience of relationship. For many, it has influenced their decision to partner or to stay single. Some have stayed single, whether consciously or not, to avoid the possible heartache of losing yet another person. Others may have gotten into a relationship expressly to diminish their risk of becoming HIV positive. (Although an understandable motivation, such a reason for forming a relationship does not lend itself to developing a strong foundation.) Still others may have stayed in a relationship far longer than they should have—sometimes out of guilt (in leaving an HIV positive partner), or fear of becoming infected (if they were then thrust into the single's world), or of ending up alone.

■ ■ ■

Gay men lack both appropriate and sufficient relationship models within this subculture. Without healthy relationship models to emulate, we gay men can often find ourselves adrift, trying to figure out relationships as best we can with no map or compass to guide us. It doesn't help us to try to use the heterosexual model, since it doesn't appear to be working very well for straight couples. More than 50% of marriages will end in divorce which does not include couples that stay together in unhappy unions.

Gay men must create a model of relationship that is internally based rather than externally derived. Each couple must determine what works for them and create a structure based on each person's needs, attitudes and expectations. With good reason, gay men should be cautious about trying to model their relationships after a straight paradigm, but the question remains: Where are the healthy gay relationships?

There is a lovely book, entitled *Men Together,* which features a number of gay couples and gives biographical essays on each, talking about how they live and love, where they came from, and what they dream of. Books such as this bring us great hope that healthy gay relationships do exist, that they deserve to be validated within the context of marriage, and that they are no *less* serious—or sacred—than straight relationships.

■ ■ ■

The gay man's view of relationship can also be greatly affected by the concept of marriage. In using the term "marriage," we need to first make some distinctions: Marriage as ceremony; Marriage as institution; and Marriage as vehicle for gaining certain legal rights and societal benefits. Marriage, as a ceremony or ritual, i.e. wedding, serves as a symbol of the couple's commitment to one another. Additionally, it makes public this commitment, where families, friends, and/or coworkers can witness and be a part of the ritual. It can be a very beautiful and important event in the development of the relationship. Some men may believe this ritual to be part of their Initiation; however, gay marriage, within this context, offers the couple limited societal validation.

For heterosexuals, the institution of marriage offers them a context within which to work, define roles, and develop a sense of identity. *I am the husband, and therefore responsible for these duties. I am the wife, and responsible for these duties.* For heterosexuals, the institution of marriage serves as a container for the relationship between the man and the woman. The container, to whatever degree the couple agrees, defines the roles. In addition, the container can actually *create* the relationship. For example, some couples get married without knowing each other very well, but they are *married.* In other words, they have a definition of what their relationship looks like even before they have developed a personal relationship with each other. The structure defines the relationship.

The power and control structure, and role defining, that the heterosexual couple might take for granted, is completely different for two men. For homosexuals, there is no such container. Without the institution of marriage, gay men must, from moment to moment, define the relationship by how well or how poorly, each is getting his needs met. Straight people do this as well, but they also have the structure of the institution to rely on and to help them understand their particular roles. Although from a more negative perspective, the structure defines the relationship for them, *before* they have defined it themselves. This is increasingly causing problems in heterosexual marriages.

The *institution* of marriage might not be as important to gay men, ultimately, as the legal and societal benefits that it could offer. Without being able to legally marry, gay couples are denied many benefits afforded straight couples, not the least of which are tax and insurance advantages. As well, without marriage, gay couples remain more vulnerable to potential difficulties with inheritance and power of attorney issues. Worst of all, as long as this society continues to deny the gay community their equal right to marry, gay men will have difficulty taking themselves and their relationships seriously.

■ ■ ■

Sex addiction greatly impairs a gay man's ability to find and sustain a meaningful relationship. If a man is an unrecovered sex addict, he will have little chance of developing an intimate relationship with another man. If he's a recovering sex addict (meaning in an active recovery process of therapy *and* 12-step work), he has greatly increased his chances of healing himself. In time, he may learn how to make the shift from his experience of years of anonymous sex with countless partners to healthy sex with one partner.

When a man has had hundreds or even thousands of sexual partners throughout his lifetime, it requires a Herculean effort to break this pattern of promiscuity and settle down with one man for the long run. As a matter of fact, Anne Schaef goes so far as stating in *Escape From Intimacy*, "I do not find that that process [sexual addiction] really is looking for intimacy. In fact, I believe that sexual addiction is a way of actively avoiding nurturance and intimacy" (p. 34).

Although the era of sexual liberation of the '70s and '80s was enormously important to the psychological and political development of gay men (in terms of breaking out of the chains of oppression that bound them), it has had some seriously detrimental consequences on their ability to be in long-term relationships.

One of the "lessons" gay men seemed to have learned from this era was to be able to have sex whenever, however, and with whomever they chose. There was value in this liberation, but unfortunately, on a collective level, some have mistaken such "freedom" for a destination. In fact, it is just another stop along the way.

High levels of promiscuity will not assist a gay man in eventually finding a partner. In becoming sexual with another man on the first date or within the first hour of meeting him, a gay man is engaging in the most intimate physical activity before ever establishing any type of foundation for friendship, safety and trust. If a relationship develops out of such an encounter, it is *in spite of* their having been immediately sexual—not because of it.

When two gay men are immediately sexual, they have eliminated an entire process of courtship and the gradual getting-to-know-each-other that could have helped them build that foundation. If they decide later on that they want to become more than just casual boyfriends, they will have to back up from that place of deep sexual intensity, in order to create a foundation for true intimacy. That backtracking can be really tricky, for it requires doing things in reverse. Instead of moving from friends to lovers, they'll have to move from lovers to becoming friends. Sometimes that's possible; a lot of times, it is not.

■　■　■

Many gay men separate friendship from love, friend from lover. How often we've heard men describe a close friend by saying, "He's my best friend. We have so much in common and it's so easy to be with him, but I don't want to be sexual." Well, why not? If you share similar values with this person, who just happens to also be gay, then maybe "Mr. Right" could be your best friend.

The truth is there is no one perfect partner for any one, but there might be a number of people out there who could be a close-enough match. If you are *reasonably* sexually attracted to a man, you share a *similar* world view, you enjoy *many* of the same things, the relationship is dynamic, *and both of you are willing to work on your issues*, is there any reason this relationship couldn't include a more intimate, romantic, sexual dimension?

■　■　■

Many gay men, motivated by their *Puer*, are imprisoned in the Knight-in-Shining-Armor fantasy in which they believe that there's this one beautiful (and perfect) man somewhere out there who's going to sweep them off their feet. They'll ride off into the sunset and live happily ever after. Sound familiar? If it does, our advice is, forget it. The prince doesn't exist. It's all myth, and gay men can spend years living in this myth and totally missing out on their life in the process. Why not develop a relationship with a human being instead? He may even be someone you already know.

■　■　■

Learning to work with conflict is tantamount to living as a Warrior in a relationship. This includes: understanding why conflict happens and what purpose it serves; learning the value of anger and how to express it in a way that could ultimately enhance the relationship, rather than destroy it. Let's take a closer look at this area.

LEARNING HOW TO WORK WITH CONFLICT

The Warrior understands how to work with conflict in a relationship. Conflict includes disagreements, arguments, heated discussions, and fights. He realizes that conflict can be a healthy and necessary component of an intimate relationship. Without this understanding, a gay man (driven by his *Puer*) is doomed to cycle in and out of relationships always looking for Mr. Right—that fantasy man whom he longs to live with conflict-free. He may spend years searching for him, and in the end find himself very alone, without the slightest clue as to what led to his predicament.

If two men are to live in a dynamic, powerful Warrior relationship, such a conflict-free state is unrealistic. Some couples we've met (even ones who've been together a long time) report that they never fight or even disagree. Maybe their definition of conflict is different from ours, certainly some of these men are in major denial, but whenever we hear this, we are somewhat stunned. We find it difficult to believe that such a conflict-free state can exist indefinitely between two men. Unless these couples know something that we don't (and if so, they need to be writing their own book), what we know is that when men couple, if they want to have a relationship with depth and vitality, there is going to be conflict.

More often, when there is a problem in a relationship, it will have more to do with conflict-avoidance than with the conflict itself. True, a conflict will need to be resolved for the relationship to improve, but it won't happen by wishing it away or pretending that it will just magically disappear. Conflict-resolution is an active process that requires participation by both partners in order for it to be successful.

From a sociological perspective, males by their nature—gay or straight—are conditioned to be more dominant than females. This conditioning, unless we are conscious of it, can pose potential problems for men loving men. Invariably, when two men form a relationship, they will eventually run up against power struggles that straight couples or lesbian couples do not. If both men are strong personalities and have control issues (which most gay men do), then the potential for conflict will be even greater.

The challenge, when men have conflict, is *not* to avoid it; rather, to learn how to work through it and come to a greater understanding of what needs, emotions, and desires were creating the conflict. Working with conflict is more than just resolving it. It includes an acknowledgment that conflict is okay and a necessary component of any dynamic relationship—especially a relationship between two men.

For a gay couple, acknowledging that conflict is okay and an acceptable facet of their relationship, helps give them permission to be at odds. They know that even though they are moving through emotional rapids, it doesn't mean that they are incompatible or that the relationship is wrong. It just signifies that they are trying to figure something out. After they've figured it out (whatever *it* is), they will invariably feel closer and more loving.

We are often asked the question, "How have you guys been able to stay in a relationship for so long?" There are many possible answers, but one stands out. We have learned how to work with conflict, which includes minor disagreements, major power struggles, differences of opinion, heated arguments, and in those rarer moments, all out war.

In the beginning we were not as adept at working through conflict as we are now. Then, we were more apt to try to annihilate each other, and later feel hugely remorseful. Now, we are more skilled at fighting fairly. That is, we have ground rules that we follow. We communicate, as clearly as possible, our anger and *not* our rage; and we stay with the process until we've made some progress toward reaching a resolution.

One of the most serious conflicts we have faced as a couple is our need to be in control. This need is not unique to us, as many gay men show signs of being "control freaks." From an even broader prospective, men in general are taught to be in control. Our control issues can center on relatively petty and unimportant things. For example, if we're driving somewhere (and usually Jim will be in the driver's seat because this is a way that he likes to feel in control), each of us will have a very clear idea of the most expedient way to get from Point A to Point B. And, of course, each of us will be right.

Whether male gay couples experience a greater amount of conflict compared to straight or lesbian couples, the jury is still out. But one thing is certain, when two men form an intimate relationship, there's a 99.9% chance that there's going to be conflict eventually. What will most likely determine the prognosis of that relationship will be the couple's ability to work through conflict, not back away from it. Additionally, they must learn how to communicate in a way that neither gets annihilated and both feel a sense of resolution. It doesn't matter what the issue is—whether it is sex, money, work, an affair, power and/or control—working through the conflict is crucial.

McWhirter and Mattison, *The Male Couple*, define the first stage in gay relationships as Blending. Somewhere between 6 months and 2 years, when this first stage is ending, conflict will more likely begin to occur. The honeymoon is over and perhaps, for the first time, things are not flowing smoothly. Each partner has begun to make his needs more known— whether verbally or more covertly—and there is static on their frequency.

When conflict arises, many gay men fail to understand its value. They may believe that there is something inherently wrong with the relationship—that it is somehow flawed, and that a "better" relationship would not include such an unpleasant experience. They may interpret its presence as a harbinger of doom, and conclude that the relationship won't be able to withstand the pressure and strain, that they are "falling out of love." Sometimes they will seek therapy; more often, they will move on, missing an opportunity to create a truly intimate relationship. These men fail to understand the importance and purpose of conflict.

It is imperative that two men in a loving relationship learn how to fight fairly, to step into the ring when necessary and duke it out. John Bradshaw says that healthy families are bloody. He is not talking about physical violence or verbal abuse, nor are we. "The ring" we're referring to is a metaphor for the place where the Warrior does battle. It is where he defends and protects himself and stands up for his truth, even when that means being very angry with his partner.

Learning to fight fairly is another integral component of the Warrior relationship. This includes establishing rules on what's acceptable behavior in times of a heated conflict and what's not. It requires learning how to be in anger and not in rage. A therapy office is a good place to work on rage; the home is not. Rage can quickly tear apart the fiber of a relationship, leaving the rageful one feeling ashamed and remorseful, and the other, the object of the rage, feeling mistrustful and unsafe, or worse, annihilated.

Following is a guide to help couples learn how to fight fairly and find their way through conflict.

One:	State the conflict.
Two:	Know that underneath the surface of every conflict or problem, there's an underlying issue needing to be addressed.
Three:	Create ground rules (For example: You can be angry, but you can't move into rage).

Four: Let each person have equal time to talk about
             his position. While that happens, the other has
             to listen and not talk.
Five: Use the formula: When you do that, I feel this.
             (Example: "When you ignore what I want, I feel
             really hurt").
Six: Know that the issue might not get resolved the
             first time around. And if this is the case:
Seven: Have an agreement that the issue will be re-explored
             after an appropriate length of time.
Eight: Take a limited Time-Out if necessary.
Nine: Accept that each person is entitled to his
             truth.

Certainly, one of the most difficult realms of any relationship is that of conflict. Learning to work through conflict in healthy and non-destructive ways is essential to the future of all relationships. In our families and within this culture, we are seldom taught the difference between anger and rage. Learning about the value of anger, and differentiating it from rage, is essential in learning to work with conflict.

THE VALUE OF ANGER

In order to learn to work with conflict, the gay man needs to understand the value of anger and be able to distinguish it from rage. Learning how to do this is a function of the Warrior. Anger, as we have already discussed, is the emotion that protects us. It is generally the result of some personal need or boundary being violated or unrecognized. Anger can be expressed directly or indirectly. All too often, gay men, who have not learned how to express their anger in a healthy and direct manner, will do so by expressing it unconsciously or indirectly—through passive aggressive behavior or bitchy sarcasm.

Conflict most often occurs when one person's needs are in opposition to the other's. There is a variety of conflict styles that men use, and it's important to learn which style(s) they gravitate toward, why they choose them, and whether or not they work. Consider for a moment what your particular behavior is in dealing with conflict: avoidance, combat, withdrawal, arguing, silence, defensiveness, or victimization.

In a conflict situation, the main feeling present is usually anger. It is important for gay men to figure out how they feel about being angry, what their "relationship to anger" looks like. For many, the concept of one's relationship to anger can be somewhat confusing, if not entirely unknown. Whatever such a relationship looks like, the work is to become an observer of how you behave when conflict arises so that you may be able to resolve conflict more effectively with your partner.

Questions to help you better understand your relationship to anger are:

- How was anger expressed when I was growing up?
- Was it expressed or suppressed?
- How did my parents resolve conflict?
- Was I allowed to be angry as a child?
- Do I allow myself to be angry now?
- What have I been really angry about in my life?
- Am I finished being angry about that event or at that person?
- Is there any part of me that likes being angry?

- Does being angry help me to feel empowered?
- Do I shut down when I find myself in a conflict situation?
- Am I overly combative at times?
- Is the feeling of anger a familiar one?
- Do I shy away from conflict or want to flee?
- Do I become invisible?
- Does conflict frighten me?

As children, we learned about anger and how to deal with conflict (or avoid it) by watching our parents navigate the white waters of their own relationship. We most likely developed a style of conflict resolution in response and/or in reaction to what we perceived to be our parent's relationship to anger and conflict.

Anger and rage are two completely different emotional states, and it is imperative that we learn to differentiate between the two. If we do not, we will tend to move in and out of either state, never knowing where the line is.

Anger is directly proportional to the severity of the event. Anger is neither good nor bad, although many of us learned that it was a "negative" emotion to be avoided at all cost. In fact, it is the feeling that most effectively protects us. It allows us to say to our world, *I will not tolerate such disrespect!* or *Get back, stay away.* Our anger helps us to establish boundaries; without it, we can easily get steamed-rolled, taken advantage of, used, or even abused.

Rage, on the other hand, is a response of such magnitude and energetic intensity, that it has very little to do with what's happening in present time. Rage is almost always about the past and is never proportional to the current event. Barring extraordinary circumstances (rape, a mugging, an accident, or war, incidents that can warrant such out-of-control emotional states), rage is not about what's going on in the moment. Instead, rage is the result of the lifetime accumulation of unexpressed, unprocessed anger that has built up like a reservoir of energy. When a person moves into rage, he is tapping into this reservoir and responding in a way that is out of proportion to what the immediate situation warrants.

Once people move into rage, violence often follows. Violence—whether it is physical, verbal, psychological, or energetic —happens when someone moves out of his own personal space and invades another person's space. When violence happens, things get broken, bodies get hurt and/or psyches get damaged. Whether the violence is physical or mental makes little difference. Rage and violence wreak havoc in a relationship; they erode the foundation by creating an atmosphere of mistrust and danger. A good place to work through rage is in a therapy office, with a therapist who is trained in deep process work and is able to maintain safety for the client, himself, and the physical surroundings. A bad place to work through rage is in a relationship.

Many people, especially those who grew up with a "rageaholic" parent, often don't realize that anger and rage are not the same. A rageaholic parent will move from anger to rage to violence in seconds, without warning, creating terror in the child. Through this, the child learns that his world is unsafe, unpredictable, and chaotic. In such a rage-filled environment, a child begins to confuse anger, rage, and violence, and will make erroneous decisions about anger (having confused it with rage) that will later shape how he responds to conflict.

At best, in such families, the line between anger and rage is very blurred, and at worst, nonexistent. If there is no line drawn between these very different emotional/behavioral states, the child will most likely conclude, *If that's anger, I don't want to have anything to do with it.* Such a conclusion will force the child to split off from his own anger. He will create a tight lid for its containment that will cause him to internalize or "stuff" it. Additionally, he may vow, even if unconsciously, never to be like his rageful parent(s). The consequences of such a vow, however understandable, are potentially disastrous for the gay man. This issue becomes exacerbated for one of the *Puer* types, the Good Boy. This type of personality learned to suppress anger at all cost, especially if he lived in a rageaholic environment. Feelings need to be expressed—all of them, not just the ones that our society deems to be "good" ones.

■ ■ ■

We gay men seem to carry an inordinate amount of anger. As with any oppressed group, our need for equality has been unrecognized, and our boundaries have been violated repeatedly over a lifetime. Unlike most other oppressed groups, gay men do not experience a sense of sameness with their families, preventing them from being able to commiserate with them. Thus the abuse we suffer, and resulting anger, has less opportunity to be periodically discharged. This can create a highly pressurized emotional state for gay men.

As well, one of the gay man's survival strategies, being the Good Boy, results in his splitting off from anger. "Splitting off" means disowning or compartmentalizing a piece of one's emotional self by stuffing this energy—in this case anger—into a box and locking it shut deep within oneself.

When anger is expressed in an indirect way, whether it's through bitchy, lacerating humor or passive-aggressive behavior, it will lead to very little significant change in one's life. When the message is unclear, there is very little chance that it will be understood. Chronically angry people are generally those who have never learned how to express anger correctly; their anger comes out in indirect ways and then they feel hopelessly misunderstood. Passive aggression keeps people stuck in their anger—where it is constantly recycled but never resolved. It is anger that is passive rather than active, indirect rather than direct, silent rather than spoken. We must learn to express anger in a healthy, direct way so that we can move anger through us and be done with it, rather than allow it to remain unexpressed and toxic. The passive aggression that is not even recognized by the angry person is the most insidious. That's the person who maintains, "Why, I'm not angry," when it is obvious to everyone around that he is.

Some people who resist expressing anger maintain they do not want to live as angry people. Ironically, this is exactly how these people end up living, since they don't express it appropriately. They are angry all the time, whether overtly or covertly. The healthy thing to do is *express the anger in order to be rid of it.*

When anger is expressed in a healthy and direct way, this action can lead to both a greater sense of personal power and a higher degree of protection. Healthy anger expression increases self-esteem because it demonstrates that one feels good enough about oneself to demand something from the world. Also, it helps one move from a place of victimization to empowerment.

Victims have great difficulty expressing their anger clearly and directly (which is one reason they are victims); empowered adults have no problem doing so. Anger expression, when done correctly, can help a relationship deepen and become more intimate. It is imperative that gay men learn how to express their anger directly to each other and to their world in order to feel more powerful.

One of the criticisms leveled against the *expression* of anger is that there is the potential for endlessly dwelling on or recycling the same anger. However, such a condition is not really about working *through* the anger, but merely allowing the anger to fester and stagnate, thus remaining unresolved.

From the Buddhist perspective, the Dalai Lama, in keeping with his philosophical beliefs, advises people not to become attached to their anger, but to allow it to flow through them. However, Jack Kornfield, a well-known Buddhist and spiritual teacher, says that many American therapists believe that this advice sounds more like encouraging people to "stuff" their anger, rather than working through this emotion. How does a person allow the anger to flow through him? We believe it is accomplished by expressing the feeling, and in that way, the anger flows through. Kornfield goes on to say that the Dalai Lama, after hearing from therapists in this country, has begun to change his position slightly and agrees that there may be times when it is appropriate to express anger.

HEALTHY DEPENDENCE

Healthy dependence is another important Warrior practice. Healthy dependence means being able to depend on other people to give us a hand and shore us up when the going gets rough. Healthy dependence is about being able to say to someone we care about, "I can't do this task alone...I need your help." Or "I'm really struggling right now. Can you come and be with me for awhile?" Healthy dependence is also about surrendering. This type of surrendering is not about *giving up*, but rather *giving in.* Admitting to that other person, *I need you in my life.* For those of us who were brought up to be good little soldiers on the emotional battlefield of life, the notion of surrendering might be synonymous with defeat. Ironically, surrendering to someone else paves the way for true intimacy.

One of the most difficult challenges we face as therapists is helping gay men learn the value of healthy dependence. When we talk to gay men about this kind of dependence, it can sometimes appear as though we're speaking a foreign language. Gay men sometimes perceive dependence as an anathema, something to be avoided at all cost. Often, these men have not considered that such a thing is possible, let alone necessary, for a relationship to succeed. Through therapy, they can learn that it is not only acceptable but appropriate for them to depend on us to be there for them and to offer them our truth.

The Codependency Movement that took the country by storm in the '70's and '80's may have, in part, shaped our views of dependence. This recovery movement helped millions of people identify a type of dependency that is both addictive and destructive to family systems, relationships and individual growth. Leaders in the movement, John Bradshaw, Terry Kellogg, Melody Beattie, and Claudia Black, helped us to understand our own codependent patterns and gave us tools to replace such patterns with healthier ones. In all, this movement helped raise the consciousness of our society and saved many lives. However, this movement was not so much a destination in terms of inner healing, as it was an important step along the way.

In codependency recovery work, we may have lost sight of the value of healthy dependence—or interdependence—the form of dependence that is not only healthy but absolutely vital for the well-being of the individual, the maintenance of communities, and the sustenance of relationships.

■   ■   ■

There is a sociological component, as well, which has shaped our view of dependence. As men, we have been conditioned to be independent, self-reliant, and autonomous. The *value* of this conditioning is that it creates highly competitive, hard working, and resourceful men. The *problem* with this conditioning is that it fails to teach the qualities that foster interdependence—vulnerability, tenderness, and compassion.

As Martin Levine, *The Gay Macho*, explains, "All men in our culture, regardless of future sexual orientation, learn the male gender role and sexual script...Families, schools, and churches teach all boys...how to be manly" (p11-12). Sociologist Janet Saltzman Chafetz includes the following characteristics in her list of traditional masculinity: virile, provider, sexually aggressive and experienced, unemotional, stoic, intellectual, rational, practical, dominating, independent, demanding, individualistic, aggressive, competitive, uninhibited, and success oriented. It is possible that gay men do not exhibit some of these characteristics as strongly as heterosexual men; gay men nevertheless have been acculturated in essentially the same way. Most of these are not qualities that make for intimate relationships.

Levine explains that girls are sexually socialized differently from boys. Girls are taught an emotional laden, relational, and procreative sexual role model. Boys are mostly socialized by their peers, thus the audience for role performance (sexual performance) is the peer group. Unfortunately, the peer group does not do a very good job of teaching sexual behavior; therefore boys fall back on their previous socialization, gender role prescriptions. In this way they see sex as a conquest, aggressive and dominating. Additionally, their sexual encounters will be devoid of emotional content and will be seen as erotic success and physical pleasure. But there is a fundamental difference between how straight and gay boys develop on these lines.

As heterosexual boys mature and come into increasingly more frequent contact with girls, they undergo a sexual resocialization that replaces recreational roles with relational ones. As gay boys mature, according to Levine, they do not go through this same resocialization and their sexual scripts remain undiluted by feminine conditioning. "In this sense, gay men may remain more fully committed to the [traditionally] masculine sexual scripts of early adolescence, more fully wedded to nonrelational, nonprocreative, and fully recreational notions of sexuality than are heterosexual boys" (p.20).

Not only have we received the same early conditioning as straight men, but additionally, our gayness has heightened our sense of independence. Our survival depended on it. The young gay boy, knowing about his differentness, learns early on to depend on no one. Being different from his own family, he cannot even rely on them for support. Our sense of differentness and lack of safety to talk openly about that differentness showed us that it would be very risky to depend on anyone other than ourselves.

In some ways, we gay men have become paragons of independence. All the ingredients are present for such a recipe. Consider for a moment: We're men, we often lack strong ties to our family of origin, many of us live alone, and few of us have children. How is it then that the gay man learns about healthy dependence when all his life, he's struggled to be as independent as possible for his survival?

■   ■   ■

In a men's group several years ago, one of the members, Mark, showed an intense dislike for another member, Rob. Mark explained that he was repelled by Rob's neediness. It took Mark awhile to realize that his strong reaction was a result of Rob's mirroring his own level of neediness. We explained that this word "neediness" could be interpreted in a different way from its usual pejorative connotation. Neediness could refer to the depth of one's longings and unmet expectations. The degree to which one comes across as needy could be proportional to the degree that such longings and expectations have gone unmet.

When asked how he could own the projection, Mark's first response was that he had to make some big changes in his life, so that he would no longer be so needy. Mark had split off that piece of himself that contained his neediness. He had developed a facade that included hyper-masculinity, fierce independence, and an emotional distance. Mark believed that his goal in getting healthier was to become as independent as possible—financially, emotionally, and physically—in order to create a protective shield from the potential dangers in his world. He believed, erroneously, if he became independent enough, he would be free.

Freedom through independence is only a half-truth. We must also experience healthy dependence to be truly free. Independence, alone, can lead to isolation, disenfranchisement, and loneliness. In time, Mark began to find new ways to deal with his neediness that included learning to depend on other group members, even Rob.

Mark is not unique in projecting his neediness outward. Many gay men are needy—they have deep and far-reaching emotional needs, many of which are not only unacknowledged, but have never been met. Their need fulfillment was thwarted because they were prevented from passing through normal developmental stages.

MONOGAMY VS. NON-MONOGAMY

Within the realm of the Warrior relationship, a gay man will at some point confront the issue of monogamy. Monogamy, and more specifically non-monogamy, are sexual behavior patterns which continue to intrigue, perplex, and often confuse gay men, whether in a relationship, or not.

No matter how much these issues are talked about, we often end up with more questions than answers. Questions such as:

- Is monogamy a realistic expectation within a gay relationship?
- How can I stay monogamous with my partner over the long run?
- If my partner and I become non-monogamous, are we honoring the sacredness of the relationship?
- If we stay monogamous, are we merely buying into the heterosexual paradigm?

Such questions are valuable and necessary to ask, but they often lead to confusion and uncertainty as to how to proceed in a relationship. Let's begin by looking at the research.

According to the authors of *The Male Couple*, "all couples with a relationship lasting more than five years incorporated some provision for outside sexual activity in their relationship." The data about monogamy and being gay, based on scientific research, is that if two men remain in a love relationship long enough, there's a good chance that they will at some point engage in sexual behavior with someone other than their primary partner.

Interesting findings. Since this study, published first in 1984, some critics have taken issue with its limitations—namely that the study was conducted in the beginning years of the AIDS crisis, before a lot of gay men had begun to seriously reevaluate and change their sexual behavior. Additionally, the study group was made up primarily of white, middle- and upper-middle class gay men in southern California. Points well taken, but nevertheless, such findings are worthy of our attention.

McWhirter and Mattison's study suggests that we need to broaden our perspective on the issue of monogamy since most gay couples they interviewed, who had been together for a long time, were not exclusively monogamous. Even though 16 years have passed since their study, and the AIDS epidemic has forced many gay men to reexamine their sexual behavior, we speculate that the patterns within gay relationships are not that much different today.

Their findings point to some important questions:

- Should long-term monogamy necessarily be what we strive toward in gay relationships?
- Must non-monogamous behavior always be viewed as dysfunctional and therefore inherently counterproductive to a relationship?
- Does such behavior indicate a diminished level of commitment within the relationship?
- Could non-monogamy suggest other possibilities as well?
- Could it be an indicator of a couple's ability to trust and respect each other at some profound level?
- Could there be such a thing as healthy non-monogamy for gay couples?

Several factors seem to hinder us from gaining a deeper understanding of this debate. One: many gay men seem to view the issue in a black-and-white fashion: *Monogamy being the "right" path and non-monogamy being inherently the "wrong" one.* Such either/or thinking leaves little room for alternatives that could be found somewhere in between these extremes.

Two, we often get side-tracked by focusing on the monogamy issue when what we're really needing to explore are the more core relationship issues such as trust, honesty, and mutual respect.

Three, we are products of an extremely puritanical society. Due to the religious and societal taboos regarding non-monogamous behavior, and because we live in a sexually repressive society, we have never learned that there could be such a thing as healthy non-monogamy or to be able to distinguish that from unhealthy non-monogamy.

Monogamy can serve some very important purposes. We believe it is essential in the early stages of a relationship in order that there be a foundation of trust and safety built. We strongly encourage new couples to practice monogamy in order to ensure the long-term success of the relationship. New relationships require great care and attention. That is not to say that established ones do not, but new relationships are more fragile, less able to weather the storms and challenges of life. Thus, they need all the help they can get—this should include an agreement of monogamy. The more a couple can focus on each other in the first years, the greater the relationship's chance of survival. Non-monogamy early on needs to be a red flag for difficulty in commitment, fear of intimacy, and possible sex addiction.

With this being said, let us continue. Monogamy vs. non-monogamy remains for many gay men a seemingly irresolvable issue. Often we perceive the issue through the lens of the *Puer*. The *Puer* prefers to view his world in a black and white fashion; ambiguity is not his favorite place to hang out. Believing that both monogamy and non-monogamy may have their place within a gay relationship may require tolerating too much ambivalence, which is clearly an adult function and not a *Puer* function. We observe that many gay men have a rather naïve outlook on relationships. They are still in an adolescent stage of development and romantically believe that if they find "Mr. Right", they will never want to have sex with another man again.

There seems to be a lot of judgment in the gay world against those men in committed relationships, who, nevertheless, allow more plurality in their sexual experience. Such judgment can include perceiving an "open" relationship as having less value, as the couple not being as committed as those who adhere strictly to monogamy. Such judgment can also include an unwillingness to relate personally to such a situation. *I would never allow my partner to be sexual with someone else.*

The gay couple that decides to be monogamous is faced with one of two choices. They have sex only with each other for the rest of their lives, *or at least for the rest of the relationship's life,* in which case, they may call themselves monogamous, no matter how much they may want to explore their sexuality with someone else. Or they have sex with other people and do not talk about it with each other, adopting a certain version of the *Don't ask, Don't tell* credo.

Society, for the most part, has some definite negative judgments about non-monogamy. Even the vocabulary we use regarding non-monogamous acts—cheating, having an affair, being unfaithful, acting out—is very revealing. Where is there room within this thinking, as indicated by our choice of words, for non-monogamy to be anything other than negative? We may need to rethink the language we use, if we want this to be a part of our experience.

This negative view extends into the realm of psychotherapy and 12-step programs. Most therapists and addictions counselors, straight or gay, will interpret non-monogamous behavior as: an escape from intimacy, unexpressed anger or rage from an earlier developmental period, unresolved power and control issues being acted out, or even retaliation. It is valid for therapists to see red flags when examining this behavior. Often, these *are* the reasons that one or both men in the partnership are having sex with other men. As therapists, we often find that gay men have outside sexual experiences for all the wrong reasons.

However, assessing non-monogamy as *always* unhealthy is shortsighted, possibly heterosexist, and definitely dangerous, for it fails to take into account that the gay path is, in ways, qualitatively different from the straight path. As well, it invalidates the gay man's ability to live his life with more breadth, adventure and fullness—some of the rewards and benefits of being gay. In saying that all non-monogamous behavior is unhealthy (i.e. wrong) in all cases, therapists are, also, buying into the black-and-white perception of the issue—*monogamy is the healthy behavior and the only way to be in relationship, and non-monogamy is unhealthy and needs to be corrected.*

If we believe this, we may have bought into the straight model of relationship. There, monogamy has served some very valuable purposes—namely to help keep family units intact and for this purpose, monogamy has had extreme value.

Judging people as wrong because of non-monogamous behavior misses the mark in all cases. Sometimes a gay man has sex with someone other than his primary partner for right and healthy reasons. He may feel a deep sense of love for that other person and want to add another dimension to their friendship. Perhaps he and his primary partner are unable to have sex due to health issues. Whatever the reason, we need to separate out what is healthy sexual exploration and experimentation with another man from what is unhealthy sexual behavior.

Furthermore, we may be talking about the wrong issue entirely. Instead of monogamy, what we really need to discuss are trust, honesty and mutual respect, and how those qualities affect a relationship. How much do I really trust my partner to stand by me? Will he leave me for someone else, or will I leave him, if we explore other people sexually? The answer: maybe. But the real issue here is about trust. Trust that the commitment of togetherness is strong enough to carry the couple through.

It takes tremendous trust on the part of both men to venture openly into the realm of non-monogamy. Without trust, the relationship is on very shaky ground. How do we build trust? The best way to begin is by getting very honest about what each other's sexual and emotional needs are. What are our sexual fantasies? How are we afraid of sex? What do we do to avoid intimacy? What are our sexual hang-ups and fears? How many of these needs are being met within the primary relationship?

What if the couple has found a deep level of intimacy and feels a tremendous sense of care for each other, but some of these needs are not being met? Does it mean they have to break up in order to find a more sexually compatible partner? Maybe, but maybe not.

Such an investigation requires a profound level of trust and honesty within the relationship. Sometimes it is difficult for a couple to discuss the realm of their sexuality. To listen to what your partner needs from you and to figure out whether you can give it; to know what you need from him, express it and listen to the response; this is some of the hardest terrain to navigate in a relationship.

Monogamy may not be for every couple. Even if it's something that works in the beginning, it may be something to be reevaluated in time. A rule of thumb, if monogamy is working for you, stay with it. It's certainly one less thing to complicate a relationship. If staying monogamous is not working, let your partner know. Nothing can change in a relationship until you're both aware of what's really going on.

In the event that one or both partners begin being sexual with other men, it is a good time for the couple to examine their relationship more closely. Outside relationships don't have to mean the end of the primary one. If the issue is worked with correctly, it could represent the beginning of a new developmental stage for the couple. It could be the very opportunity they have needed to move to a deeper level of understanding of themselves, each other, and the relationship. Sometimes the help of a trained professional is necessary, but it is important that he or she has enough objectivity about this issue to be of help.

Some gay couples have an agreement that it is permissible to have sex with somebody else provided he is a stranger, and that it is not talked about. We believe this type of agreement presents a certain set of complications. First, in having sex with a stranger, one increases the chance of exposure to some type of STD. Second, in not talking about an outside relationship from the onset, a pattern is begun which includes mistrust, dishonesty and deception —qualities that do not lend themselves to building intimacy. Intimacy breaks down when there are secrets being kept; it is enhanced when our deepest longings, fears, and dreams are revealed. Having sex with another man may actually enhance the primary couple's relationship, if the couple is being honest about it.

Some couples opt to bring a third person into their relationship. Sometimes threesomes are limited to what happens in bed among the three men, but it could evolve into an on-going and vital three-way relationship. This is relatively rare, but there are those men who are experimenting in this realm. Some appear to be making it work. They are the pioneers of uncharted territory and a reminder to us all that there are many different ways to love and live. Let us not limit ourselves to only one model. We are so much greater than that.

Non-monogamy means different things depending on the couples' level of commitment to each other and length of time they've been together. We separate non-monogamy into two distinct categories: Unhealthy and healthy. Unhealthy non-monogamy refers to sex addiction, a flight from intimacy, unresolved power and control issues, and/or unexpressed anger. Healthy non-monogamy, on the other hand, can be present only when there is a deep level of trust and commitment in the relationship.

Relationship agreements can become brittle and obsolete if they are not reviewed periodically. As the two men in a partnership grow and change, so does the relationship. Rules that might have once worked may no longer serve the couple. Even if the couple agreed, in the beginning, to be monogamous, they may need later on to discuss if such an agreement is still viable and beneficial. Perhaps some new agreement might be more advantageous to them then.

It could be that gay men have a need to express themselves sexually in some fundamentally different ways from heterosexuals. This may include having sex with someone other than one's primary partner at some point in the relationship? Whatever a couple decides in terms of monogamy, it is vital that they learn how to talk with each other about sexuality, i.e. sex, dreams, desires, longings, and fantasies. Also, they need to remember that coming to an agreement requires listening closely to one another and speaking from the heart.

In summary, if a gay man is truly committed to finding a partner and developing a long-term Warrior relationship, he must experience an Initiation. Whatever its particular form, it will require him to separate from his family of origin and take the other necessary steps that will allow him to become his own person, freed from the constraints, power, and control of his parents and the rest of society.

When a gay man allows for and is able to work through periodic conflict in his relationship, he is embracing the Warrior. When he learns how to express his anger in a healthy way, knowing that this is essential to being a powerful man and partner, he is living as a Warrior. We are not promoting anger expression for the sake of making gay men angrier. Rather we are suggesting ways for them to get this energy out of their bodies, so that they can make room for more enjoyable emotional experiences.

Gay men need to acknowledge the forces that work against being able to find and sustain healthy, intimate relationships. They need to look at how they start their relationships. Relationships that begin immediately with sex have the least chance of surviving over the long run. Taking it slower, making it a process, can greatly enhance the chances of finding a healthy, sustainable partnership. Gay men all too often make intimacy *an event*, by having sex right away. True intimacy is actually *a process* that takes many years to achieve. This process can require re-learning some old, often times commonly accepted beliefs about sex and relationship.

BECOMING POLITICAL

The historical challenge for modern man is clear—to discover a peaceful form of virility and to create an ecological commonwealth, *to become fierce gentlemen* (italics ours).
— *Fire In The Belly*, Sam Keen, p.121.

For the gay man to live as a Warrior, he must become political. The first step to becoming political is in coming out. Coming out helps him to protect his personal interests as well as adding to the strength of the larger gay community. Even though coming out may, in the beginning, lead to a feeling of vulnerability and over-exposure, in the long run, such information actually helps protect him. He is saying to his world, "This is who I am. If you vote against equal rights legislation for gay people and if you support anti-gay politicians, social or religious groups or organizations, then you are voting against me."

Another step to becoming political is to vote—in both national and local elections. To vote effectively, the gay man needs to determine which Party he's going to endorse. To do so, he will need to stay informed and know who the candidates are who support gay issues. Of the two major political parties, is there really a choice? One can certainly find fault with the Democratic Party's track record when it comes to gay legislation, but all one has to do is look at the voting record of the Republican Party to see that they consistently vote against gay issues.

If we look at current political trends, it's hard not to see the power of the Republican Party's anti-gay agenda, fueled by the ever-growing Christian Coalition, which in time may have far-reaching and potentially disastrous consequences for the gay community. The Christian Coalition, whose doctrine bears little resemblance to that of Christ's teachings, has spent the last ten years successfully infiltrating school systems across the country and could soon create the biggest educational reform in the history of our country. If this reformation were to take hold, issues such as social tolerance and acceptance of diversity would not be found in any of their curriculum guides. Instead, they would be permitted (using our tax dollars) to teach their children the evilness of homosexuality. From Newt Gingrich, to Jesse Helms, Pat Buchanan, Ralph Reid, and Trent Lott, these Republican politicians support and vote for anti-gay legislation. At every opportunity, these men desecrate the word democracy.

As these issues continue to heat up, all gay Americans will be challenged to step onto the political stage to fight for their civil rights. Rights that a certain growing number of fear-based and bible-thumping Republican homophobes are more than ready to strip from gays and lesbians once and for all. Clearly, the single most important civil rights issue of this new century will be that of equal protection legislation for our community. If we do not focus as much of our attention, money, and energy on this issue as possible, the Republican Party may succeed in keeping us from attaining equal rights for another decade or more.

To be gay and a Republican could be one of the more blatant forms of internalized homophobia and an example of aligning with the oppressor. The argument that gay Republicans are trying to change the Party from within can sound well intentioned, but underneath, it may point to a high level of denial. For many people the Republican Party has come to represent bigotry and oppression in a similar way to that associated with some organized religions. Gay Republicans need to question whether they are out of touch with their righteous indignation and are committed to being Good Boys, thus unable to realize the detriment to themselves. The gay Republicans whom we have met seem to base their partisan standing on one main issue—economics. How can protecting one's financial holdings justify endorsing a Party that has worked so hard to strip us of our rights; that continues, at every turn, to keep us a second-class citizenry?

Even if the argument is sound from a political perspective, we are looking at the issue from a psychological one—the mental health of the individual. Maybe the Log Cabin Republicans *can* effect change in the Republican Party, but what are the consequences for the gay man's psychic well-being?

■ ■ ■

Another step toward being political is talking about politics with other gay men, women and *heterosexuals*. It helps us formulate our ideas and become clearer about what we truly believe, and it helps others to know us better. In so doing, it is possible that we may learn new ideas that we hadn't previously considered.

As therapists, we encourage our clients to talk about politics as another way to heal. Although such a therapeutic strategy would be *verboten* within a more traditional therapeutic setting, we have learned that encouraging men to talk about their political beliefs is a very significant part of their therapy. We see a deep need in gay men to exchange ideas with other men about political issues, and to be able to express their feelings (passion, fear, skepticism, indifference and excitement).

James Hillman speaks extensively about the value of discussing politics (and religion) in therapy. What are your beliefs and why do you believe them? What are your reasons for being a member of a particular Party? Where do your beliefs come form; are they merely remnants of your parents' teachings? Are they *Puer* beliefs or are they Warrior beliefs? These are all important questions that should be addressed in therapy. We should be able to defend our reasons for our beliefs and to be open to new ideas about them.

Sometimes we hear a gay man say, "I'm not very political." Often this is a result of his feeling alienated by a system that has sought to keep him oppressed. When we hear this, we encourage him to consider what such a statement means, and if it's really true. It is possible that he is already being more political than he realizes.

Being political teaches us to take a stand. If a gay man is out, then by virtue of his outness, he is being political. That is to say, to be political as a gay man, one is required to be out. Conversely, being out is being political. By the very nature of a gay man saying he is gay, he is committing a political action. He is taking a stand and declaring to his world that he wants to be recognized for the whole person that he is.

Another step to becoming political is joining a gay organization. There are many such organizations doing great work to make our lives better: Human Rights Campaign, (HRC), The National Gay and Lesbian Task Force, (NGLTF), Lambda Legal Defense, and Parents and Friends of Lesbians and Gays (PFLAG), to name a few. Becoming a member brings one more immediate access to what's going on in the world and offers a more direct connection to the people who are on the front lines, creating more freedom and safety for the rest of us.

In summary, to be strong gay men, it is imperative that we become political. This includes: coming out; voting; staying informed; talking about our beliefs, rather than remaining silent; and joining a gay political organization or starting our own. By telling our world the truth about us, we help people know that we are everywhere and that we are as diverse as the rest of the population. Being political is about having opinions and expressing them. As writers, we have had to risk that we might offend some of our readers, but we can't let that fear prevent us from expressing our truth. If we did, we would not be modeling Warrior behavior.

WARRIOR WORK

Following One's Bliss

To return the sense of dignity and honor to manhood, we have to stop pretending that we can make a living at something that is trivial or destructive and still have a sense of legitimate self-worth.
— *Fire in the Belly*, Sam Keen, p.168.

When a gay man learns how to use work as a vehicle for expressing his passion, he is living as a Warrior. The Warrior understands the value of work. He knows that work, if it has true meaning, serves a purpose greater than just enabling him to survive. It allows him to feel more complete—intellectually and emotionally—and more connected to his world.

Joseph Campbell talked of the importance of "following one's bliss." Bliss is the state of being of joy and contentment. Campbell was saying that if we figure out what we most love to do, and then follow that love or "bliss", we will eventually find our true life work. Life work can be as diverse as the number of people on the planet. It is work that maximizes our potentiality and is in harmony with our inner nature, best expressing our uniqueness.

Work can be looked at in one of two ways, through the lens of the *Puer* or the Warrior; either as something we have to do in order to survive, or something we want to do because it gives expression to our soul's purpose, respectively. The first is W.O.R.K.—a four-letter word that is often gray and lifeless; the second suggests a full spectrum of color through unlimited creativity and joy.

For some gay men, work is one of those necessary evils that must be endured, so that the rent can get paid and the car not repossessed. These men put in time every week at a job that they do not like, biding their time until the weekend when they can get back to their "real life." For others, work offers them an opportunity to express their vast creative potential while getting paid to do so. Gay men, living as Warriors, find joy in what they do; the division between work and free time is not as well defined. There is a world of difference between these two types of work.

Many men spend their entire lives at jobs that do not satisfy them. They do so because they believe they have no other choice. Perhaps they saw their fathers working in jobs that were soulless and have concluded that this is how work is meant to be experienced. Maybe their self-esteem is damaged enough that they feel they do not deserve to be happy in their work. Whatever the reasons, these men are the tragedies of the modern age.

The Industrial Revolution did much to influence men's perceptions of work. First, the factories took men away from their families. Next, it taught them that working 40 (or more) hours a week, 50 (or more) weeks a year was, not only necessary, but also the *right* thing to do. Last, it stripped men of their ability to express their own creative yearning. The factories—not their hearts—dictated what would be produced. This began the dehumanization of men in the workplace. Men learned specific lessons: work was not about enjoyment; its physical demands would age them before their time; and maybe they'd have a few good years of retirement before they died. Today, many of us carry these same perceptions of work that were passed down by our fathers.

We are now in a transitional period. The Industrial Age has not fully ended, and the technological age is still forming. Alvin Toffler speaks of the many changes that are taking place during this time in his book, *The Third Wave*. Even though this book was written in 1980, the concepts are still very relevant. We remain in the transition phase between the second and third wave of civilization. This transitional time creates great challenges for us.

The most well adjusted men that we've met are those who love their work. For those of us who *have* to work, it makes sense that we should find work that we really love. We spend a big chunk of our life doing it—approximately 2000 hours a year. That's far too much time to spend doing something that we hate or feel ambivalent about.

■   ■   ■

Our story is a good example of two men's search for meaningful work. We were both teachers before becoming therapists. The allure of three months off each summer (which for ten years, we spent in Mexico and Central America) and eventual retirement, kept us in those careers far longer than was healthy. The years went by, we continued to teach; not really loving what we were doing, but satisfied enough. All the while, each of us had a nagging feeling that there was a different kind of work beckoning us.

It took us some time to pay attention to that calling, but finally our dissatisfaction with teaching grew strong enough that we knew we had to leave. Certainly teaching is a very respectable profession, but in most parts of the world, one must remain closeted to be a member of that profession.

We left teaching and the community where we had lived for many years. We said goodbye to the security of regular paychecks and a good retirement plan. After living in Spain for almost a year, we moved to New Mexico and entered graduate school to study psychology. Still, we didn't know where this new journey would lead, but we believed this further education could help us find work more compatible with our emerging identities—out gay men.

Breaking away from the familiar and venturing into the unknown required taking some big risks. Had we not taken those risks, we would have never found our true life-work. At times along this journey, we were certainly afraid. Other times, we questioned whether we were doing the right thing. The questioning and the fear were as much a part of the process as the desire and exhilaration of a new direction in life. We knew that so long as we didn't let the fear immobilize us or the questioning deter us, we'd eventually find what we were looking for.

After finishing our degrees and doing several years of in-patient psych work, we decided to open our own practice. There we began to work with gay men and soon realized that this would become one of our specialty areas. After all, it was what we knew best; it was the kind of life work that we had been longing to do. Our work had evolved into helping gay men heal. In turn, this helped each of us undergo a deeper personal healing. How blessed we feel in having finally found our life work.

As an example, a client was feeling deep grief about having lived for many years in secrecy and shame about being a gay man with HIV. One day, while deep in his sadness, he looked up and said, "Don't you get tired of watching me cry? You must be really bored with all this." I thought for a moment about his question and the incredible courage that I had witnessed in this man week after week, and I told him, "There's no place I'd rather be than with you, right now, as part of your healing. I feel very honored." I wanted him to know that through his courage and commitment to his work, he was helping me to love *my* work all the more.

■　■　■

How does a gay man find his life work when he may not know where to begin to look? First, he might want to spend some time in a quiet place contemplating what he really enjoys doing. He could do this in meditation or while on a walk in the woods. When his mind is at rest, he can begin to notice where it drifts. These moments can reveal what his unconscious mind is trying to communicate to his conscious mind about his true path. Sometimes the information might appear in the form of illness or depression, which could be the psyche's way of getting his attention when all else fails.

Scott came to see us several years ago. He was a successful lawyer who had recently been experiencing a deep depression. Whenever asked about his work, he invariably reported that it was going along "just fine," but Scott rarely showed much interest in talking about it any further. One day, he came to session after an aerobics class and his energy was decidedly changed. He spent the entire session talking about how much he loved movement and how he had always wanted to be a dancer.

When he was a child, his mother had taken him to see the ballet and from that moment he knew what he wanted to be. His father, on the other hand, discouraged Scott's interest in dance and insisted that he study something "practical." Now, Scott lamented not having pursued his love of dance, but added that his father was probably right—"It wouldn't have been very practical. I do have to make a living."

Over time, Scott immersed himself in his law career and forgot that he had ever wanted to be a dancer. Not until he was in his mid-forties, and in the throes of a successful career, had he started to experience this nagging sensation (that came in the form of depression), reminding him of something very important that he had lost along the way.

Scott's story is not an uncommon one. Over the years, we've heard many variations on this same theme. It points to one of the main reasons why so many people have difficulty finding their "bliss"; it was taken from them at an early age. Scott's father was not an evil man, but he clearly had not helped Scott nurture a deep soul longing. Instead, he encouraged his son to forsake his own desires for his. Scott's need to please his father outweighed his ability to hold on to this soul longing—to be a dancer.

A good gauge of one's bliss is when work and the other aspects of one's life become indistinguishable. Often when we have free time, we'll find ourselves exploring the same issues as in our work with clients. There is a fluidity that has developed, where we no longer see work as what we do solely at the office and leisure as what we do when we're off. Another indicator of meaningful work is not wishing time away while on the job. When there is joy in work, there is less need to be somewhere else; therefore, the passing of time becomes less important. When one feels as free in the workplace as he does at home, the search for one's bliss is complete.

THE GAY ELDER

...Man, like no other animal, not only knows that he is
killing when he kills but also knows that he too will die;
and the length of his old age, furthermore, is—*like his
infancy—a lifetime in itself, as long as the entire span
of many a beast.* (italics ours)
— *The Flight of the Wild Gander,* Joseph Campbell, p. 110.

To age gracefully we must aspire to become wise and
beautiful elders.
— *Fire in the Belly,* Sam Keen, p164.

When a gay man lives as a Warrior, he not only understands the value
of the elder, but also consciously prepares for his eventual role as one. In
American culture, there are few elders. We know some exist, for periodically
we have the good fortune of crossing paths with them. Sometimes we read
their books and know by what they tell us that they are elders. Men like
Robert Bly, James Hillman, Sam Keen, John Lee, Scott Peck, and Joseph
Campbell are some good examples of elders.

In gay culture, there is an even greater absence of elders—strong, older
gay men living as warriors. This is a sad situation for us all, for we live in
a culture that does not value aging. Instead, we tend to discard the elderly.
This undervaluing and discarding of the old is even more pronounced in
gay culture. One has only to pick up a gay magazine to see how obsessed
we are with youth.

Older gay men we've worked with often report feeling alienated and
isolated from younger men. A 70-year-old client of ours once said in group,
"When I'm at the bar, I feel invisible. Younger men look right through
me...as if I didn't even exist." This is a sad, yet not surprising, commentary
on gay culture. Until we begin to see the tragedy of this situation, we will
continue to overlook the precious resource that older gay men could offer
the younger ones.

Let us look for a moment at what it means to be an elder. An elder is someone older who offers guidance and direction to someone younger. In indigenous societies, elders hold a special place of honor and respect. They are revered. They pass on the traditions and the history—they are the keepers of the culture. What's more, they help the young move from a place of adolescence into adulthood; they are integral to the initiation process.

To be a gay elder, a man must be more than just old, he must also be wise. He needs to have an acceptance of the aging process and understand its value. As well, he has learned to grieve the losses incurred along his journey—the loss of his youth, perhaps the failure to have accomplished certain goals, or the deaths of friends and partners. He allows himself to feel the depth of his suffering and yet chooses to go on. Here's what Sam Keen has to say about wisdom:

When we think about the nature of virility, we need to ponder the difference between a smart man and a wise man. It seems that smart men think abstractly; wise men think autobiographically. Smart men remove themselves from the problem about which they are thinking; wise men bring all of their experience to bear. Smart men think quickly, with the conscious mind; wise men slowly simmer and allow the unconscious to play. Smart men live in the moment and believe any problem that can be defined can be solved; wise men recollect the past and respect the perennial limits of the human condition. *Smart men are usually young; wise men are usually old.* (italics ours) (p. 162).

There is a number of reasons for the dearth of gay elders in today's society. In a collective sense, we are still in an adolescent stage of development. This is evidenced by what we most value. We tend to place highest value on youth and beauty, and often look at older men as having less value. We are obsessed with working out, staying thin, pumping up and looking 25 when we're 45, and 40 when we're 60.

Because of our youth-driven mainstream culture, which is only intensified in gay culture, many gay men have an aversion to growing older. Through media, we learn that aging is something to be avoided at all cost. We become imprisoned in our own obsession with youth. Rather than gaining more personal power as we progress through life, we surrender our power to the ideal that youth is ultimately more important than knowledge.

Men who come out later in life have much to grieve. They might have been married for years with families, and grieve the loss of a life (no matter how inauthentic) in which they invested much time and emotion. They often feel a profound sense of loss, and have difficulty finding other gay men who can empathize with them. Not only do they feel the loss of all those "wasted years", but also the loss of the person they may have spent many years believing they were. Whatever the reason for one's grief, in order for a man to become an elder, it is essential that he identify his losses and learn how to grieve them.

Today's older gay men did not have elders in their formative years to show *them* the way; they did not have books such as this one suggesting the value of elder-status. They grew up in an age when homosexuality was regarded as pathology—by society, the medical establishment, and by the gay community itself. They certainly could not look to the society at large to offer them support, but neither could they find it within much of their own community. Even though we still live in a homophobic, and at times, homo-hating society, most gay people have gained enough self-esteem to know that homosexuality is not pathological, but a normal variation on the human theme. Older gay men did not grow up with this same understanding.

In the book *Cures,* Martin Duberman describes how he was finally able to accept his gayness, *despite* all the years of treatment. Because he believed that it really was a disease, he spent many years in psychoanalysis in an attempt to be "cured" of his homosexuality. Duberman's account is not just an autobiography; it is an historical testament. For gays of Duberman's era, life was very different; and that was not so long ago.

The belief that homosexuality was a sickness prevailed through the 40's and 50's. The Sixties began to challenge that belief, but it wasn't until 1975 that homosexuality was removed from the *Diagnostic and Statistical Manual of Mental Disorders*. Duberman's book gives us much greater insight into why the older gay men of today tend to be so out of touch with their power. Some of them actually succeeded in establishing gay relationships, but the overriding feeling was that the "self-images that we could manage in the fifties hardly made us candidates for serenity: we were pieces of shit around whom the world revolved" (p. 23). He further explains:

> But for straight couples, social values serve to counteract problems in the relationship; the high premium placed on heterosexual pair-bonding and family life provides plenty of brownie points and self-

esteem for staying together. For homosexual couples, social values serve further to underscore, rather than counteract, interpersonal difficulties; being called "sick" and "degenerate" hardly gives one the needed psychic support for sustaining a relationship (p.31).

The psychic wounding of older gay men has been profound and long lasting. Many of them have remained semi-closeted. They may be out in the gay community, but will still have straight friends whom they have not come out to. Quite often they will defend this position vociferously. They have lived this way for years and they see no reason to change at this late date. In actuality, they are not addressing their long abiding and internalized homophobia. Many members of this population have achieved a relative amount of financial success and this, too, can be a deterrent from making the changes necessary to live more consciously.

Ultimately, it is the responsibility of the individual to make peace within himself about the realities of aging. But the older gay man of today lacks the support of his peers, as well as his community, to understand what it means to age as a Warrior—to age with grace and retain one's power, or better, to let the accumulation of years increase one's personal power.

The Warrior has to face the reality that he is no longer a young man, and now must derive a sense of value from something other than having a youthful body. Such value must come, instead, from his life experience, which he can use as a source of wisdom to be shared with younger men. In this way they can know more about how their culture has evolved in the last sixty, seventy, eighty years.

It is imperative that we find men in our world who are elders, who can model for us what it means to grow old *and* be conscious. Who are the gay elders in today's society? Who are the men who best exhibit Warrior behavior? Those who most quickly come to mind are men like Martin Duberman, Richard Isay, and Larry Kramer. Others, who have died and would have been elders include: Harvey Milk, Paul Monette, and Randy Schiltz. These men, most of them writers, have shown great courage in expressing their beliefs, in being out and in not backing down in the face of adversity.

"What about all the 'wise old queens' who figure so prominently in gay life throughout the 20th century?" stated one publisher. The old queens in our history surely deserve our respect and gratitude for bucking a very homophobic system, but the word *tough* comes to mind, rather than *wise*.

One of the best places we know of for "elder-learning," and for linking younger gay men with older ones (to create mentor/protégée relationships) is group therapy. A gay men's therapy group, where there is a wide spectrum of ages, can be an excellent place to help men develop a better understanding of the importance of the elder. One such example happened not too long ago in one of our groups when we brought in a new member, a man we'll call Ben. He was in his early sixties, which made him the oldest member of the group.

Ben had recently ended a 20-year marriage, was still struggling with coming out and had already begun a relationship with another man. One evening, the group began to explore with Ben his potential for serving as an elder for the men in the group. Initially, he was pretty resistant to the idea. He tended to downplay his strengths by making statements like, "I've got way too many issues to be an elder. What do I have to teach any of these men? I was married and in denial for all those years—and a raging codependent besides!" In other words, he didn't believe he was wise enough. We explained that the role of elder could develop over time; as he continued his own healing process, he might begin to assume such a role for some of the men in the group and even men in other areas of his life. Ironically, as time went on, the more Ben resisted acknowledging his elder potential, the more the group challenged him to look at the ways he was already being that wise, older man.

As he continued his work, he began to understand and correct his codependent patterns, he grieved the loss of so many years in a heterosexual existence, and he got in touch with his deep and long-repressed anger. Through intensive work, as Ben started to give his anger a voice, he moved out of the role of victim into a place of empowerment.

Ben began to get in touch with his anger at his mother, and to set firmer boundaries with his ex-wife, who had continued long after the divorce to try to manipulate him. Additionally, he began getting very politically involved at his work—a government-run institution that, historically, had been conservative and homophobic. In fact, his involvement included participating in the company's first-ever Gay, Lesbian and Bisexual Alliance promoting diversity in the workplace. In a word, Ben had blossomed as a gay man. In the hearts and minds of the rest of the group, he had become an elder.

Being designated as an elder didn't mean that Ben had finished his work, nor that he was now enlightened, for he would probably be the first to tell you that the work is never completed. But what it did mean was that Ben had used his betrayals—the abuse of his mother (family betrayal), "wasted" years in a straight marriage (the betrayal by society, which had coerced him into accepting the straight paradigm), a lifetime of stuffing anger (the betrayal of self)—and turned them into wisdom. His *betrayals* (woundings), as he healed them, had become his *wisdom*. Now, they were rich life experiences that he could draw from in helping younger men find their way. He knew, first-hand, what it meant to have lost touch with himself for many years and then to finally rediscover that self. He knew, not theoretically, but on a visceral level, the price one must pay for trying to be someone other than who one really is.

How different Ben's life might have looked had he had a gay mentor. How different all of our lives might look...had we had someone like Ben, some older gay man working at being conscious, healing old wounds, who could have helped us find the way. Ben finally recognized that a big part of his healing was to accept this role of elder—so that perhaps a few men whom he connected with along the way could benefit from his wisdom, that they might not have to suffer quite as much, for quite as long.

He understood that a large facet of his life work was to make himself available to younger gay men (by accepting his capacity to mentor)—not to repeat earlier codependent dramas, not to care-take anyone else in an unhealthy manner—but to care for and provide healthy interdependence with men who needed him. This awareness helped increase the richness in his life and the lives of the men who were hungry for his guidance. Because he was now ready to be that elder, and because he had done enough personal work, his life and the lives of those he continues to touch are filled with more depth and intimacy.

Being an elder is a life experience available to any man who is willing to let go of the *Puer* and embrace the Warrior. With each passing year, and every additional wrinkle around the eye, we are beckoned by life to embrace this challenge, the challenge to understand ourselves as older gay men and to provide guidance and leadership. To see a gay man who is aging with grace, who is consciously embracing the changes of time, is a beautiful thing. That man teaches us, through his presence, that what awaits us does not have to be dreaded or avoided. He models for us that aging gracefully is the result of conscious living. In Victor Frankl's words: "...there is no reason to pity old people. Instead young people should envy them.... Instead of possibilities in the future, they have realities in the past—the potentialities they have actualized, the meanings they have fulfilled, the values they have realized—and nothing and nobody can ever remove these assets from the past" (p.151).

We gay men, *if fortunate enough*, will someday be old men. But just being old won't bring us elder status. To be elders, we're going to have to start now to prepare for that time when our bodies have succumbed to gravity and time, our skin has thinned and wrinkled, and our hairlines have receded. If we have done our work, we will have wonderful things to teach the gay men of tomorrow, the ones who are crawling around in diapers as this is written and the ones who have not yet been born.

To prepare ourselves for that time, we must continue the journey to find the Warrior deep inside who can accept the aging process. We must learn how to greet each coming year with anticipation and reverence, rather than with annoyance and dread.

To accelerate this process of locating and acknowledging the elders, it is important that we begin to seek them out with clearer intention. We could use the personals or the Internet to locate each other. *Younger gay man seeks guidance of conscious gay elder*. This puts an interesting twist to personals.

To the older readers of this book, who believe themselves ready to embrace their elder status, we invite you to make your presence known. *Gay elder seeking younger gay man to mentor*. It is important to note here that a mentor relationship is usually nonsexual. When sex is introduced into a relationship, the dynamic becomes that of peers (no matter how large an age difference) and it can eliminate the potential for a mentor/protégée relationship. This is not to say that sex makes a mentor relationship impossible, just trickier to navigate.

Younger gay men need older gay men just as much as the opposite is true. The younger benefit from the older man's guidance, just as the older becomes rejuvenated by the vitality and new ideas of the young. There needs to be more of an exchange of energy between old and young gay men, so that we can learn from each other. The elders must assume their rightful place within our communities, so that the younger no longer have to find their way alone. Hopefully the elders can be the gateway into expanded awareness, showing the younger that they, too, can make it.

> It strikes me that the lack of substantial manliness one finds in some gay communities is a result not of a homoerotic expression of sexuality, but of the lack of a relationship of nurturance to the young. To be involved in creating a wholesome future, men, gay or straight, need an active caring relationship to children. A man who takes no care of and is not involved in the process of caring for and initiating the young remains a boy no matter what his achievements. (Keen, p.227)

DEVELOPING A SPIRITUAL PATH

"My gayness cannot be compartmentalized. It's not just some dimension of my being—it is my being. My gayness flows through my bloodstream, it is in my bones... encoded in my DNA. It is not just what my body wants to do with another man's body; more importantly, it is how my heart and mind and all of my body wants to express itself."
— From a client

When one becomes a gay Warrior, one is more fully living as a spiritual being. Whenever we live in honesty and truth, when we risk being all of whom we can be, we are living as spiritual beings. Our gayness *is* our spirituality, and when we embrace who we are as gay men, we allow our spirit to shine through our humanness. The more we embrace our humanness, which in our case, is inseparable from our gayness, the more we recognize our spiritual nature.

As the gay man gets more in touch with his Warrior, as he moves through his own particular version of Initiation, he is, *at the same time*, developing a spiritual path. Developing a spiritual path is made up of many facets and some of the most important of these facets are: courage to be oneself, compassion for oneself and others, making room for fear, an understanding of the nature of suffering, living with intention, a connection to the earth, finding a sacred place, learning to be still, and the importance of giving back.

Being oneself is about not compromising one's integrity and uniqueness for anyone at anytime. It requires breaking through all the barriers of shame and fear and self-loathing that keep us from really embracing our magnificence. A good example of someone modeling this behavior was the young gay man in New Jersey who decided to take his boyfriend to his senior prom. Against great pressure, he was determined to be himself.

Compassion begins with self and extends out to one's world. It is an understanding of why we struggle, and that struggling doesn't necessarily mean that we're doing anything wrong. More often, it simply indicates that we're experiencing the difficulty of being human. Compassion includes allowing ourselves to feel afraid without judging. Integral to the human condition is fear. It is imperative, when we are frightened, that we treat ourselves with compassion.

One of our group members, Patrick, was castigating himself for not having come out in a recent situation. He was in a Spanish class and his instructor asked him if he was married, and why not and did he have a girlfriend. He so wanted to tell the instructor, and the rest of the class the truth, but suddenly he was frozen with fear. In recounting the experience, he lamented that he had been such a coward.

What happened to this man was not cowardice; it was fear. Our fear of rejection is not just imaginary. Our fear that something bad might happen to us if people knew the truth is not unfounded (Consider Harvey Milk and Matthew Sheppard). *Bad things can happen to gay people.* The odds are that, when we come out, nothing bad *will* happen, but sometimes it does. Violence can be exacted on gay people. It happens a lot more than we probably care to acknowledge.

So why wouldn't we have fear? Our work is in figuring out how to break through the fear, not to beat ourselves up for having it. This requires a depth of compassion for the difficulty of the gay path. This is not to invoke pity, nor to imply that gay people have a corner on suffering, but to remind ourselves that it's been a rough road. Whether it is coming out, or finding a relationship, or feeling truly like a man.

Stillness helps one to be in the present moment. It is found when we allow the world around us to stop. It's about jumping off the train that many of us seem to be riding, taking us to those supposed important destinations—success, power, fame, prosperity, enlightenment—and breathing in the clean, crisp air of Now.

There's only one thing required to finding stillness. One must be willing temporarily to set aside all commitments, activities, demands, pursuits, distractions, obligations, and begin to pay attention to what is occurring all around, now. Stillness can be attained anywhere, at anytime for anyone. It is free. It is available to us all. Few in this society allow themselves to enjoy such a precious gift. A gift whose worth is beyond calculation. You don't have to travel thousands of miles to find it, there's nothing to pack, and dress is optional.

A common method of stilling the mind is through meditation. Some people are intimidated by this concept. They may think that they have to join a temple or "sit" for hours a day or they may think of it as something very foreign. It doesn't have to be any of these things. Meditation is becoming increasingly more common in our culture and here is an easy way to approach the practice.

Sit in a comfortable chair or sit on a pillow on the floor. The point is not to torture yourself, but to be comfortable. It is important that you sit upright with your head and back straight, your eyes closed and completely quiet. Choose a specific place and time of day for your meditation. The type of meditation that we are suggesting is called "empty mind meditation." The idea is eventually to learn how to empty your mind, so you will be able to open what is closed, balance what is reactive and explore what is hidden (Goldstein and Kornfield). Jess Lair calls it holding hands with God. The God of your choice.

While trying to empty your mind, you may use a mantra or you may concentrate on your breathing. You can use anything you want for a mantra, such as: Ham-so (I am that), or religious names, Jesus, Yahweh, or you can count your breaths, whatever works. You will notice that when you sit down to meditate, all the things that you need to be doing will surface. Just say to yourself, "resistance," and continue meditating. Jack Kornfield suggests that when you are distracted by a noise or thought, say to yourself, "distraction," or when you realize that you thinking about something, say, "thinking." In this way you allow the thought to exit your mind and then you come back to your mantra or breaths. It will take time to learn to meditate, but it will not take long to be able to feel your body relax.

Try to meditate for twenty to thirty minutes, once a day to begin with. At first you may want to use a clock, but after awhile, you will develop an inward clock and you will have a pretty good idea how long you've been sitting. When you are ready to quit, keep your eyes closed and stretch your hands above your head, then slowly open your eyes and sit quietly for a minute.

Stillness brings us home. We rediscover our essence and return to that place that spiritual teachers call oneness. We find that place deep within where our truth resides. Stillness takes us to our center, to the core of our being, where we find our creative juices, our particular brand of passion, our unique vision of the world. It is a place that, when found, offers the finder a state of deep peace, of profound relaxation and well-being.

Slowing down our world is a task that many of us have difficulty accomplishing. In fact, if it is viewed as a *task*, something to accomplish, we're already on the wrong track. We are so accustomed in western society to having to do something to get what we want. Stillness is all about not doing. Not doing anything. Just being.

It might be about sitting in a comfortable chair looking at a bird, perched on a branch, singing softly; or gazing at the buildings across the street and hearing the sounds of traffic on the busy street below. It could be about sitting on a beach, watching a crab scratching a trail through the sand or tracing the flight pattern of a pelican flying a few yards from the shore; or lying on the cool, damp grass in early autumn watching a squirrel run past with a mouthful of acorns. These are examples of stillness.

Think back to the last time you allowed yourself to be totally still. Maybe you had the flu and had no choice but to stay in bed. You might have tried watching TV or reading a book, but eventually, when those things no longer worked, you had no choice but to just lie there and be still. What did you think about? Were you okay with just being or did it bring up uncomfortable thoughts—loneliness, sadness, or boredom?

Why is it so difficult for many of us to be still? One, we don't understand its value, and two, we are geared toward being human "doings" instead of human beings. We work in order to produce, so that we can be valuable members of society; people will respect and admire us, thus we get approval, recognition, and accolades. Stillness is the antithesis. We do it *not* to get anywhere, but to stay right where we are, so we are able to take in the magnificence of what's before us.

Spirituality also includes connecting to the earth. Much of the dis-ease in our world is the result of people having lost touch with the natural world. Without a connection to nature we are spiritually bankrupt. With it, we will never be alone—we'll have a great companion called Earth. In connecting to the earth, we allow ourselves to see it as a living, breathing organism. When we see the earth as a part of us, we're much less apt to hurt it—throwing a cigarette out the car window; not recycling; supporting uncontrolled, ill-planned development; or condoning toxic waste. Caring for the earth is a spiritual practice.

How does one re-connect with the Earth? First, if you live in a city, get out of it as often as you can. When you can take a drive out into the country, park your car, get out and walk on the earth, whether it's at the beach or in a forest or on the desert. Swim in the ocean, sail on a lake, canoe down some river. Whatever you choose, be in nature, and let it teach you about what's really important. There is a poem from a northwest Native American tradition that might help explain this concept:

Lost
Stand still
The trees ahead and bushes beside you are not lost.
Wherever you are is called, here.
And you must treat is as a powerful stranger.
Must ask permission to know it,
And be known.
Listen—the forest breaths,
It whispers, "I have made this place around you.
If you leave it, you may come again, saying, 'here,' just, 'here.'"

No two trees are the same to raven,
No two branches the same to wren.

If what a tree or branch does, is lost on you—
Then, you are surely lost.

Stand still; the forest knows where you are,
And you must let it find you.

For each of us, it is vital that we find a place on the earth that is sacred. A sacred place is where we find safety and refuge from the every day world. Sacred places are most commonly found in nature, but sometimes they exist within the heart of a big city. Some of the sacred places we've found along our journey would include: inside a ring of ancient redwoods in Muir Woods; on the mesa top of an Anasazi ruin; the cathedral in Santiago de Compostela, Spain; and Chichen Itza in Yucatan, Mexico.

A sacred place offers us a transcendent experience, helping us to feel the presence of god or reminding us more fully of our inextricable link to the rest of the world and to the cosmos. Ancient peoples knew the importance of sacred places; indigenous peoples throughout the world still do. Many of us living today have forgotten.

A spiritual activity that we recommend is therapy. In therapy we work to become more conscious. The more conscious we become, the more we are in touch with the world around us and the better able we are to care for the world and those who live on it. God (whatever your definition) is often defined as Truth. Gandhi said, "I am a passionate seeker after truth which is but another name for God." Those brave enough to enter a psychotherapist's office are seeking the truth, thus they are seeking God. In Scott Peck's words:

> Those who come to psychotherapy are the wisest and most courageous among us. Everyone has problems, but what they often do is to try to pretend that those problems don't exist, or they run away from those problems, or drink them down, or ignore them in some other way. It's only the wiser and braver among us who are willing to submit themselves to the difficult process of self-examination that happens in a psychotherapist's office.

What could be more spiritual than embarking on a voyage to the innermost recesses of our being? A voyage to make the unconscious, conscious and to bring our shadow selves into the light, to transform our deepest wounds into an endless source of compassion, strength and wisdom. This is the journey of the Warrior.

PART VI

CONCLUSION

The gay American must find hope for life that does not deny the cultural and social realities of life, but acknowledges them...the realities of our lives must be included in any paths we find to travel. False paths, paths that deny reality, ultimately lead nowhere. They will lead us from our true selves, from the ability to connect with others, and from an inner capacity to love and be loved. If paths rooted in reality lead through deep sand, or are more treacherous than we expected, then we will not travel as far in a day. If they lead to destinations other than those we expected, we must rethink our plans and our purposes in life.
— *In the Shadow of the Epidemic,* Walt Odets, p. 235.

In the past 40 years, gay men have made enormous strides in becoming more visible and empowered. The revolution began with Stonewall; it continued when homosexuality was removed from the DSM as a "psychiatric disorder"; and it was exponentially accelerated with the AIDS epidemic. Now it is time to take the next step forward in our development—to find the Warrior in each of us individually. In order to do so, we must let go of our allegiance to the *Puer,* individuate from our family of origin, and heal our betrayals that may have previously left us feeling alone and mistrusting. When we do this Initiation work, our families, our communities and society will begin to take us more seriously, and perhaps offer us the same rights and privileges afforded straight people. The responsibility will be ours to show that we deserve such things as equal rights protection; clearly, we have a lot more work ahead in fighting this battle.

We are an awesome people—a community of resilient, courageous, multi-talented, diverse individuals who know a lot about pain and suffering. If we can learn how to use those past experiences, including our betrayals, as a source of wisdom, we can become powerful teachers, spiritual guides, and visionaries to help heal this ailing planet. Don't we owe it to ourselves and those we love to discover our greatness? Finding the Warrior will help us advance further along the path to such greatness.

Being a gay Warrior is about living with honesty, passion and, when necessary, fierceness. It means not shying away from being a strong man, which is often the antithesis of the good boy. It's about learning to genuinely care for ourselves and others. It's about being out, even when that might feel like the scariest option imaginable. It requires taking lots of risks, being willing to make some huge mistakes along the way, and then taking even more risks.

Finally, it requires an enormous leap of faith that we will survive the Initiation, that we will be welcomed on the "other side" by those who have made a similar journey and have learned to be true men. As we stand on the edge of that great chasm which separates us from the deeper recesses of our masculinity, remember: it's not as wide as you think—jump.

BIBLIOGRAPHY

Barrie, J.M. *Peter Pan*. Charles Scribners, New York, 1911.

Bawer, Bruce. *A Place at the Table*. Simon and Schuster, New York, 1993.

Beattie, Melody. *Codependent No More*. Harper and Row Publishers, San Francisco, 1987.

Berne, Eric. *Transactional Analysis in Psychotherapy*. Grove Press, Inc., New York, 1961.

Bly, Robert. *A Little Book on the Human Shadow*. Harper-Collins, San Francisco, 1988.

Bly, Robert. *Iron John, A Book about Men*. Addison-Wesley Publishing Company, Inc. New York, 1990.

Campbell, Joseph. *A Joseph Campbell Companion*. Ed. Diane K. Osbon. HarperCollins. New York, 1991.

Castaneda, Carlos. *Tales of Power*. Simon and Schuster, New York, 1974.

De la Huerta, Christian. *Coming Out Spiritually: The Next Step*. Tarcher/Putnam, New York, 1999.

De Ropp, Robert. *Warrior's Way: The Challenging Life Games*. Dell, New York, 1979.

Duberman, Martin. *Cures*. Plume. New York, 1992.

Egendorf, Arthur. *Healing from the War*. Shambhala Publications, Inc. Boston, 1985.

Faludi, Susan. *Stiffed: The Betrayal of the American Man*. William Morrow and Company, Inc. New York, 1999.

Forward, Susan. *Toxic Parents: Overcoming Their Hurtful Legacy and Reclaiming Your Live*. Bantam Books, New York, 1989.

Frank, Ann. *The Diary of a Young Girl*. Bantam Books, New York, 1991.

Frankl, Viktor E. *Man's Search for Meaning*. Simon & Schuster, Inc. New York, 1984.

von Franz, Marie-Louise. *Puer Aeternus*. Sigo Press, 1970.

Goldstein, Joseph & Kornfield, Jack. *Seeking the Heart of Wisdom*. Shambhala. Boston & London. 1987.

Haley, Jay. *Uncommon Therapy*. W.W. Norton & Company. New York, 1986.

Isay, Richard A. *Being Homosexual: Gay Men and Their Development*. Farrar, Straus, Giroux. New York, 1989.

Jeffers, Susan. *Feel the Fear and Do It Anyway*. Fawcett Columbine. New York, 1987.

Jones, Alexander. *Men Together: Portraits of Love, Commitment, and Life*. Running Press. Philadelphia, 1997.

Jones, Dan. *The Roller Coaster Kid Finds His Way Home*. Mandala Publications. Austin, Texas, 1992.

Kafman, Gershen & Raphael, Lev. *Coming Out of Shame: Transforming Gay and Lesbian Lives*. Doubleday. New York, 1996.

Keen, Sam. *Fire in the Belly: On Becoming a Man*. Bantam Books. New York, 1991.

Kiley, Dan. *The Peter Pan Syndrome: Men Who Have Never Grown Up*. Avon Books. New York, 1984.

Kopp, Sheldon. *Who Am I…Really? An autobiographical exploration on becoming who you are.* St. Martin's Press. New York, 1987.

Kornfield, Jack. *The Heart of Spiritual Practice.* [Cassette recording]. Sounds True, 1996.

Lair, Jess. *I Don't Know Where I'm Going, But I Sure Ain't Lost.* Fawcett Crest. New York, 1981.

Lee, John. *I Don't Want to be Alone.* Health Communications, Inc. Deerfield, Florida, 1990.

Lee, John. *Recovery: Plain and Simple.* Health Communications, Deerfield, Florida, 1990.

Lee, John. *At My Father's Wedding: Reclaiming Our True Masculinity.* Bantam. New York, 1991.

Levine, Martin P. *Gay Macho.* New York University Press. New York and London, 1998.

Lew, Mike. *Victims No Longer: Men Recovering from Incest and Other Sexual Child Abuse.* Harper Collins. New York, 1988.

Lowen, Alexander. *Narcissism: Denial of the True Self.* Macmillan Publishing Co. New York, 1985.

Masterson, James F. *The Search for the Real Self, Unmasking the Personality Disorders of Our Age.* The Free Press. New York, 1988.

McNaught, Brian. *On Being Gay.* St. Martin's Press. New York, 1988.

McWhirter, David & Mattison, Andrew. *The Male Couple.* Prentice Hall, Inc. New Jersey, 1984.

Miller, Alice. *For Your Own Good: Hidden Cruelty in Childrearing and the Roots of Violence.* Farrar, Straus, Giroux. New York, 1983.

Moore, Robert & Gillette, Douglas. *King, Warrior, Magician, Lover: Rediscovering the Archetypes of the Mature Masculine.* Harper, San Francisco, 1990.

Mueller, Wayne. *Legacy of the Heart: The Spiritual Advantages of a Painful Childhood.* Simon & Schuster. New York, 1992.

Odets, Walt. *In the Shadow of the Epidemic.* Duke University Press, Durham, North Carolina, 1995.

Peck, Scott. *The Road Less Traveled.* Simon and Schuster. New York, 1978.

Peck, Scott. *Further Along the Road Less Traveled.* Simon and Schuster. New York, 1993.

Raphael, Ray. *The Men from the Boys.* University of Nebraska Press. Lincoln & London, 1988.

Reid, John. *The Best Little Boy in the World.* Ballantine Books. New York, 1973.

Satinover, Jeffrey. Science and the fragile self: The rise of narcissism, the decline of God. In Levin, David (Ed.), *Pathologies of the Modern Self.* New York University Press, New York, 1982.

Schaef, Anne Wilson. *Escape from Intimacy.* Harper & Row. San Francisco, 1989.

Shilts, Randy. *The Mayor of Castro Street, The Life and Times of Harvey Milk.* St. Martin's Press, New York, 1982.

Siegel, Stanley. *Uncharted Lives: Understanding the Life Passages of Gay Men.* Plume. New York, 1994.

Sparks, Tav. To hell and back: one man's recovery. In Keith Thompson (Ed.), *To Be a Man*. Perigee, New York, 1991.

Sullivan, Andrew. *Virtually Normal: An Argument about Homosexuality*. Alfred A. Knopf, Inc., New York, 1995.

Toffler, Alvin. *The Third Wave*. Bantam Books, New York, 1980.

Van Gennep, Arnold. *The Rites of Passage*. University of Chicago Press, Chicago, 1960.

Williams, Tennessee. *Suddenly Last Summer*. Dramatists Play Service Inc., New York, 1958.

Woodman, Marion. *The Ravaged Bridegroom*. Inner City Books, Toronto,1990.

Woodman, Marion. *Addiction to Perfection*. University of Toronto Press, Toronto, 1982.

YOUR PRIMARY SOURCE
for print books and e-books
Gay, Lesbian, Bisexual
on the Internet at

http://www.glbpubs.com

Through special arrangements with the authors, this book is also available as a download from the Internet for those whose access to printed books of this nature is limited. The entire book can be downloaded to your own computer from the web site above, price US$9.00, in a variety of formats to suit your choice. The direct access web address is:

www.glbpubs.com/gw.html

Additional print copies can also be ordered by mail for the US and Canada only directly from the publisher. Please enclose your check or draft as follows:

Paperback   US$ 17.95 + $4.00 s/h = US $21.95

Casebound   US$ 26.95 + $6.00 s/h = US $32.95

Mail to:
GLB Publishers, P.O. Box 78212, San Francisco, CA 94107

No overseas orders, please.

Also email at: glbpubs@glbpubs.com for enquiries.